Lars-Henrik Olsen

Tracks and Signs of the Animals and Birds of Britain and Europe

translated by Mark Epstein

Princeton University Press
Princeton and Oxford

Copyright 2013 © by Princeton University Press

Published by Princeton University Press, 41 William Street,
Princeton, New Jersey 08540

In the United Kingdom: Princeton University Press, 6 Oxford Street,
Woodstock, Oxfordshire OX20 1TW
press.princeton.edu

Originally published in Danish as *Dyr & spor* in 2012 © by
Gyldendal A/S, Denmark

ISBN (pbk.) 978-0-691-15753-5

Library of Congress Control Number: 2013931523

British Library Cataloging-in-Publication Data is available

This book has been composed in Goudy Sans and Goudy Oldstyle
Printed on acid-free paper ∞
Printed in Livonia, Latvia
10 9 8 7 6 5 4 3 2 1

Contents

A crevice used by a woodpecker to lodge a pine cone. NO.

Preface

Most birds are active during the day, and we can easily observe their activities. Mammals are shyer; many of them can be seen only at dusk or at night. They do not wish to reveal their whereabouts except to fellow members of their species, but all animals leave tracks—a footprint, a lost feather, tooth marks on a tree, a hole in the ground, a special odor, and so forth. If you learn what to look for in animal tracks and can identify them, the time you spend in the field can become even more rewarding.

This book is a window into the rich variety of bird and mammal tracks and signs. Seen in the wild, they reveal a lot about animal behaviour. When trying to identify tracks, it is obviously helpful—as well as enriching—to know something about the animals themselves. For this reason, the second half of the book contains descriptions of most species of European mammals, their habits and habitats, as well as some facts about size, appearance, and distribution.

Animal tracks sometimes tell a story. This picture shows the tracks of several animals. A **Willow Ptarmigan** *was surprised by a* **Golden Eagle***, and the eagle was lucky; it managed to push the ptarmigan into the snow, drive its claws into its victim, and fly away with its prey. A* **Mountain Hare** *and a* **Norway Lemming** *went by, either shortly beforehand or shortly thereafter—perhaps they were witnesses to the scene. AK.*

Mammal tracks

Most wild animals are very shy. Many mammals are nocturnal and rarely seen, but you can find their footprints. To determine the identity of the animal that left these tracks, size and shape are of course important, but also understanding the series of tracks in its entirety, the type of movement, length of stride, and the 'splay' of the feet, as well as the distance between the prints of the hind and forelegs. All of these will provide additional information about the kind of animal we are dealing with.

If you know something about the animal's distribution and behaviour, the place and the surroundings where the tracks were found will also provide a lot of information. If you follow one set of tracks you will often also find other signs: food remains, signs of chewing or digging, carrion, nests and other structures, droppings, and so forth—there is a lot to see.

Tracks reveal the type of movement of an animal: walk, trot, gallop, or jump. The form and sequence of the tracks can be of great help in the identification process. For most of the species in this book, the type of movement is described along with the relevant footprint.

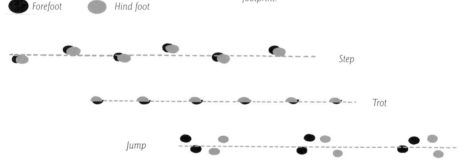

● *Forefoot*   ● *Hind foot*

Step

Trot

Jump

An example of three characteristic tracks.

The print pattern is based on the entire impression of the bottom of the foot. For mammals, we distinguish three major groups of prints: hooves of one toe, hooves of two toes, and paws with claws or nails.

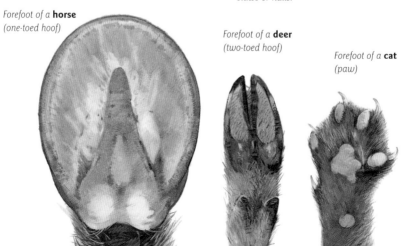

Forefoot of a **horse** *(one-toed hoof)*

Forefoot of a **deer** *(two-toed hoof)*

Forefoot of a **cat** *(paw)*

Actual size

Raccoon
Dog tracks

Raccoon Dog
See p. 127
Front foot L: 4–5.5 cm, W: 4.5 cm
Hind foot L: 4–4.5 cm, W: 3.5 cm

Domestic dog

Wolf

*Dog/Wolf
tracks*

Domestic dog/Wolf
See p. 111
Wolf
   Front foot L: 9–11 cm, W: 8–10 cm
   Hind foot L: 8 cm, W: 7 cm
Dog: varying sizes

L = Length
W = Width

Approx. two-thirds actual size

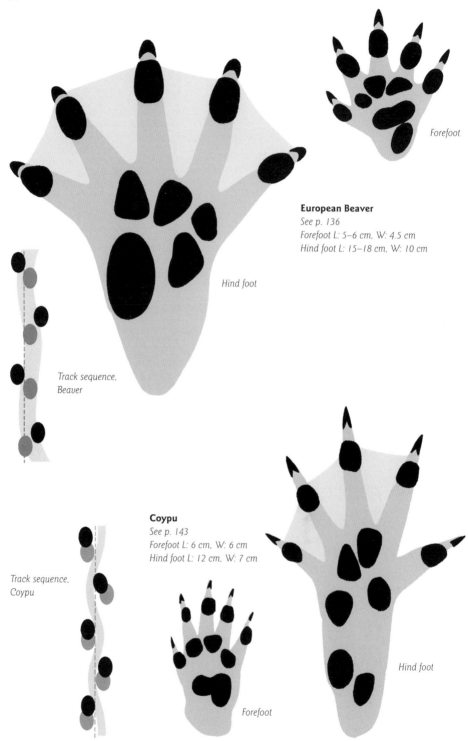

Forefoot

European Beaver
See p. 136
Forefoot L: 5–6 cm, W: 4.5 cm
Hind foot L: 15–18 cm, W: 10 cm

Hind foot

*Track sequence,
Beaver*

Coypu
See p. 143
Forefoot L: 6 cm, W: 6 cm
Hind foot L: 12 cm, W: 7 cm

*Track sequence,
Coypu*

Forefoot

Hind foot

Actual size

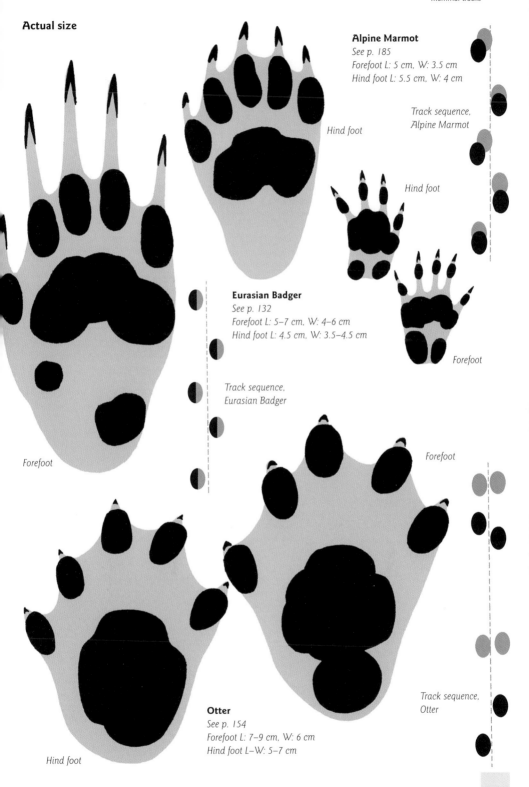

Alpine Marmot
See p. 185
Forefoot L: 5 cm, W: 3.5 cm
Hind foot L: 5.5 cm, W: 4 cm

Track sequence,
Alpine Marmot

Hind foot

Hind foot

Eurasian Badger
See p. 132
Forefoot L: 5–7 cm, W: 4–6 cm
Hind foot L: 4.5 cm, W: 3.5–4.5 cm

Forefoot

Track sequence,
Eurasian Badger

Forefoot

Forefoot

Track sequence,
Otter

Otter
See p. 154
Forefoot L: 7–9 cm, W: 6 cm
Hind foot L–W: 5–7 cm

Hind foot

Actual size

Wildcat/domestic cat
See p. 118
Forefoot and hind foot L: 3–3.5 cm, W: 3 cm

*Track sequence,
Wildcat/
domestic cat*

Lynx
See p. 115
Forefoot L: 6.5 cm, W: 5.5 cm
Hind foot L: 7.5 cm, W: 6 cm

*Track sequence,
Lynx*

*Track
sequence,
Pine Marten/
Beech Marten*

**Pine Marten/
Beech Marten**
See pp. 163, 165
Forefoot L: 3.5 cm, W: 3.2 cm
Hind foot L: 3 cm, W: 2.5 cm

*Track
sequence,
Red Fox*

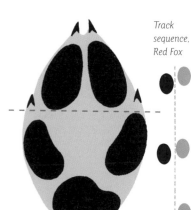

*Track
sequence,
Wolverine*

Wolverine
See p. 109
Forefoot and hind foot L: 14–18 cm
W: 10–13 cm

Red Fox
See p. 123
Forefoot and hind foot L: 5–7 cm
W: 4–4.5 cm

Varying sizes

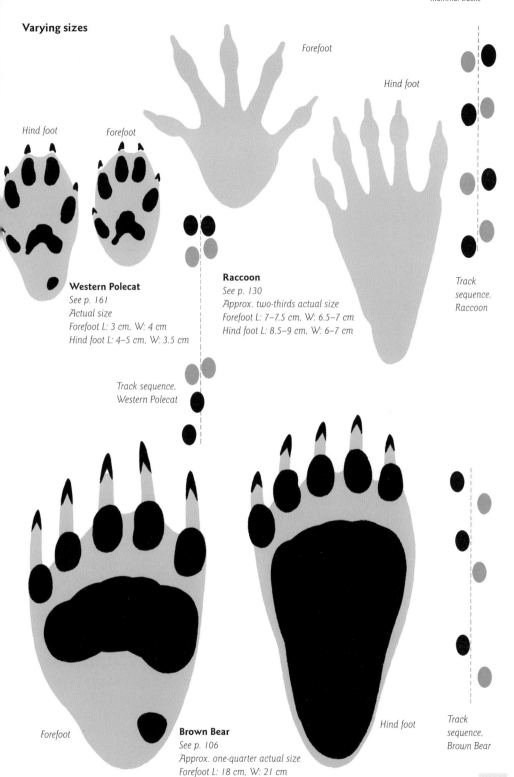

Forefoot

Hind foot

Hind foot   Forefoot

Western Polecat
See p. 161
Actual size
Forefoot L: 3 cm, W: 4 cm
Hind foot L: 4–5 cm, W: 3.5 cm

Raccoon
See p. 130
Approx. two-thirds actual size
Forefoot L: 7–7.5 cm, W: 6.5–7 cm
Hind foot L: 8.5–9 cm, W: 6–7 cm

Track sequence, Raccoon

Track sequence, Western Polecat

Forefoot

Hind foot

Brown Bear
See p. 106
Approx. one-quarter actual size
Forefoot L: 18 cm, W: 21 cm
Hind foot L: 27 cm, W: 17 cm

Track sequence, Brown Bear

11

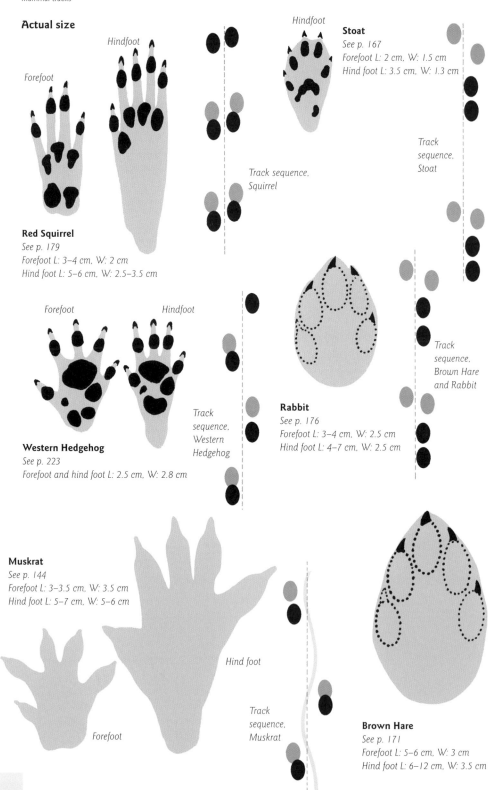

Actual size

Hindfoot

Forefoot

Stoat
See p. 167
Forefoot L: 2 cm, W: 1.5 cm
Hind foot L: 3.5 cm, W: 1.3 cm

Hindfoot

Track sequence, Stoat

Track sequence, Squirrel

Red Squirrel
See p. 179
Forefoot L: 3–4 cm, W: 2 cm
Hind foot L: 5–6 cm, W: 2.5–3.5 cm

Forefoot　　　*Hindfoot*

Track sequence, Brown Hare and Rabbit

Track sequence, Western Hedgehog

Western Hedgehog
See p. 223
Forefoot and hind foot L: 2.5 cm, W: 2.8 cm

Rabbit
See p. 176
Forefoot L: 3–4 cm, W: 2.5 cm
Hind foot L: 4–7 cm, W: 2.5 cm

Muskrat
See p. 144
Forefoot L: 3–3.5 cm, W: 3.5 cm
Hind foot L: 5–7 cm, W: 5–6 cm

Hind foot

Forefoot

Track sequence, Muskrat

Brown Hare
See p. 171
Forefoot L: 5–6 cm, W: 3 cm
Hind foot L: 6–12 cm, W: 3.5 cm

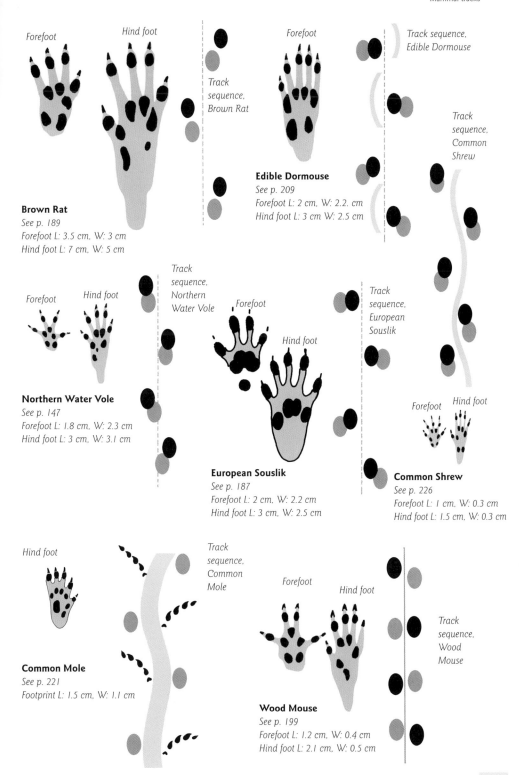

Forefoot   *Hind foot*

Track sequence, Brown Rat

Brown Rat
See p. 189
Forefoot L: 3.5 cm, W: 3 cm
Hind foot L: 7 cm, W: 5 cm

Forefoot

Edible Dormouse
See p. 209
Forefoot L: 2 cm, W: 2.2. cm
Hind foot L: 3 cm W: 2.5 cm

Track sequence, Edible Dormouse

Track sequence, Common Shrew

Forefoot   *Hind foot*

Track sequence, Northern Water Vole

Northern Water Vole
See p. 147
Forefoot L: 1.8 cm, W: 2.3 cm
Hind foot L: 3 cm, W: 3.1 cm

Forefoot

Hind foot

Track sequence, European Souslik

European Souslik
See p. 187
Forefoot L: 2 cm, W: 2.2 cm
Hind foot L: 3 cm, W: 2.5 cm

Forefoot   *Hind foot*

Common Shrew
See p. 226
Forefoot L: 1 cm, W: 0.3 cm
Hind foot L: 1.5 cm, W: 0.3 cm

Hind foot

Track sequence, Common Mole

Common Mole
See p. 221
Footprint L: 1.5 cm, W: 1.1 cm

Forefoot   *Hind foot*

Wood Mouse
See p. 199
Forefoot L: 1.2 cm, W: 0.4 cm
Hind foot L: 2.1 cm, W: 0.5 cm

Track sequence, Wood Mouse

Approx. two-thirds actual size

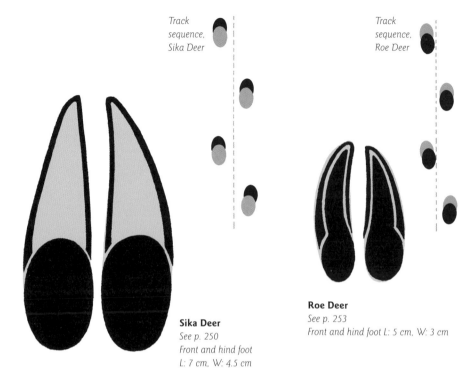

Track sequence, Sika Deer

Track sequence, Roe Deer

Sika Deer
See p. 250
Front and hind foot
L: 7 cm, W: 4.5 cm

Roe Deer
See p. 253
Front and hind foot L: 5 cm, W: 3 cm

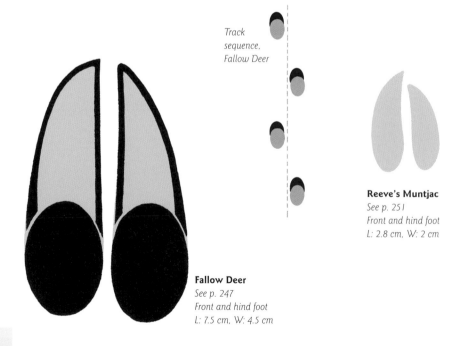

Track sequence, Fallow Deer

Reeve's Muntjac
See p. 251
Front and hind foot
L: 2.8 cm, W: 2 cm

Fallow Deer
See p. 247
Front and hind foot
L: 7.5 cm, W: 4.5 cm

Actual size

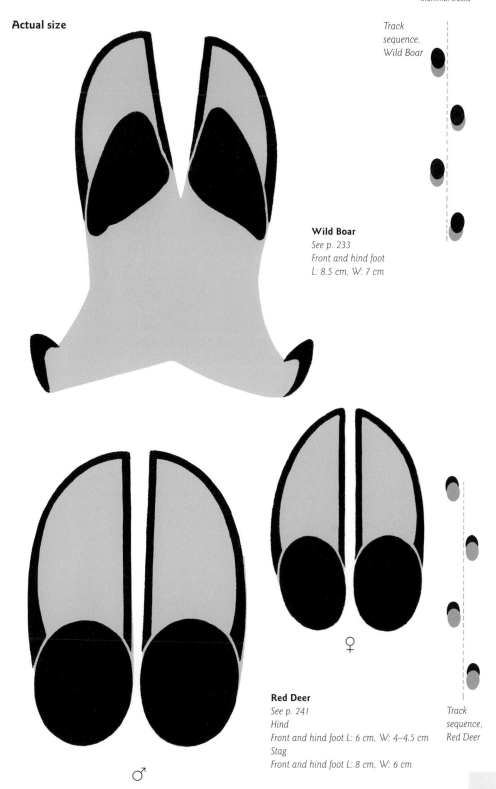

Track
sequence,
Wild Boar

Wild Boar
See p. 233
Front and hind foot
L: 8.5 cm, W: 7 cm

♀

Red Deer
See p. 241
Hind
Front and hind foot L: 6 cm, W: 4–4.5 cm
Stag
Front and hind foot L: 8 cm, W: 6 cm

Track
sequence,
Red Deer

♂

Varying scales

Track sequence, sheep

Track sequence, Mouflon

Mouflon
See p. 263
Front and hind foot
L: 5 cm, W: 4 cm

Sheep
See p. 266
Front and hind foot
L: 5 cm, W: 3 cm

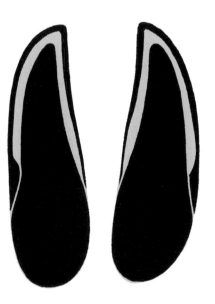

Track sequence, Elk

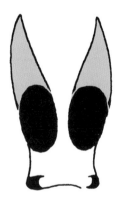

Chamois
See p. 265
Front and hind foot
L: 6.5 cm, W: 4.5 cm

Elk
See p. 237
Approx. one-half actual size
Front and hind foot
L: 12–16 cm, W: 13 cm

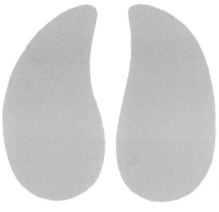

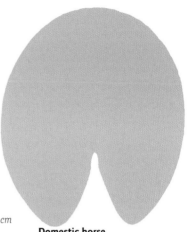

Domestic cattle
See p. 232
Approx. two-thirds
actual size
Front and hind foot
L: 10–12 cm, W: 9–10 cm

Domestic horse
See p. 231
Approx. one-half actual size
Front and hind foot L: 12–25 cm

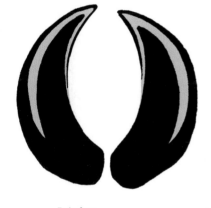

Reindeer
See p. 258
Approx. one-half actual size
Front and hind foot
L: 8–10 cm, W: 11 cm

Track sequence,
Reindeer

Domestic goat
See p. 267
Front and hind foot
L: 5 cm, W: 4 cm

Reindeer. *AK*

Antlers

Approx. one-quarter actual size

Each species of deer has a specific antler shape which is easily recognisable. Female Reindeer also have antlers, but they are significantly smaller than those of males.

An antler consists of large bone material. It grows each year from the forehead in an area referred to as the pedicle. While growing it is covered by a loose skin containing its own blood vessels, the velvet. An antler grows very fast, about 1 cm a day. Once the antler is fully developed, the velvet dies off.

Deer shed velvet by rubbing their antlers against bushes and small trees—antler-rubbing, or 'rubbing off the velvet'. Rubbing off the velvet is also used to mark a male's territory. The deer normally eat the shed velvet, which is why it is only rarely found in the field.

Antlers of **Roe Deer**.
LG.

Reeve's Muntjac
See p. 251

Roe Deer
p. 253

Elk
You can find antlers that differ greatly in shape; see p. 237

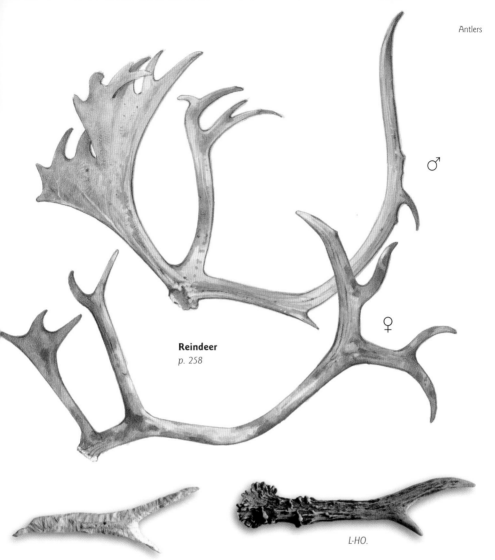

♂

♀

Reindeer
p. 258

Mouse tooth marks on the antler of a Roe Deer.

L-HO.

Shed Reindeer antlers. SS.

After the mating season, deer shed their antlers, and a new, often larger set takes their place. The shed antlers do not remain preserved for long. Numerous animals, especially mice, feed on them to get calcium. The discarded antlers will gradually disappear over time.

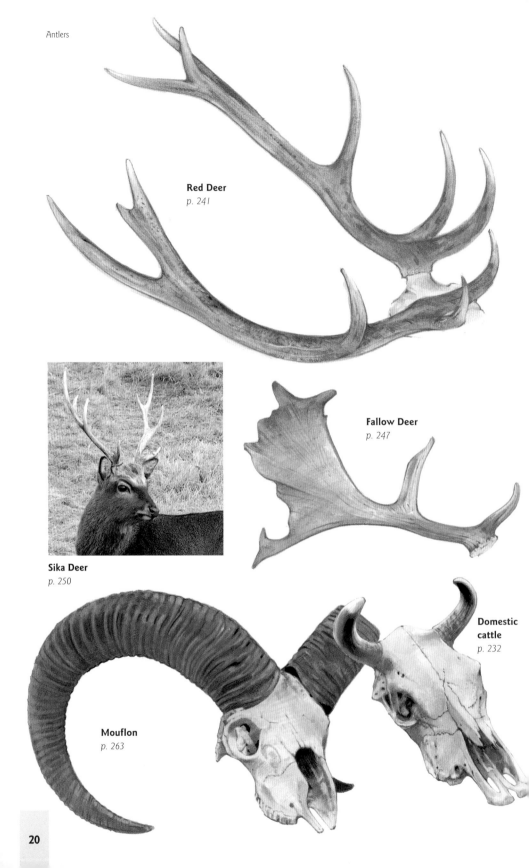

Red Deer
p. 241

Fallow Deer
p. 247

Sika Deer
p. 250

Domestic cattle
p. 232

Mouflon
p. 263

Horns are hollow and develop like claws and hooves through a transmutation of outer skin layers. Horns consist of a hollow shell on top of bone 'cones' on the head. They are usually curved or twisted, but they are never forked like antlers. They are not shed but continue to grow from the base year in, year out. This is why sections of horn closest to the skull are the most recent, while those at the tip are the oldest.

Drinking horn. AK.

Mouflon ram. MG.

*A **Fallow Deer** with plant remains in his antlers after marking his territory. JC.*

Bird tracks

Bird footprints can be difficult to identify, but different families do leave distinctive prints. We can see five bird-foot shapes here, which in addition to their characteristic marks also reveal behavioural and ecological relationships.

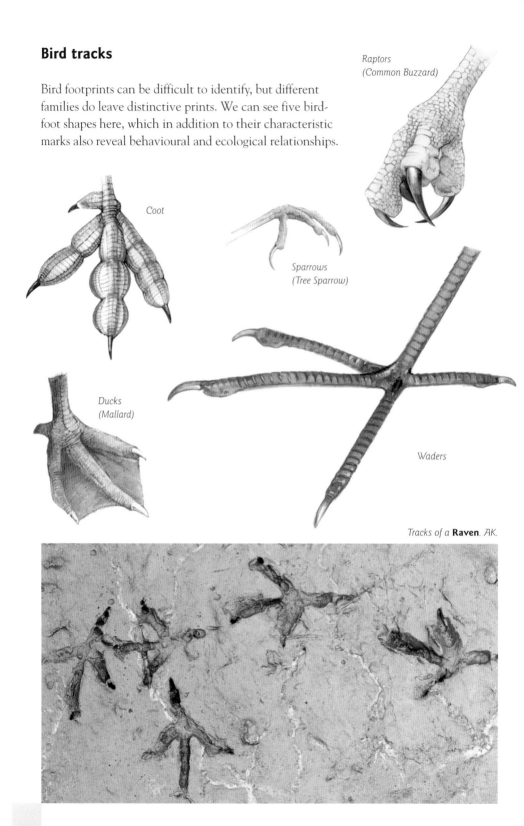

*Raptors
(Common Buzzard)*

Coot

*Sparrows
(Tree Sparrow)*

*Ducks
(Mallard)*

Waders

Tracks of a **Raven**. AK.

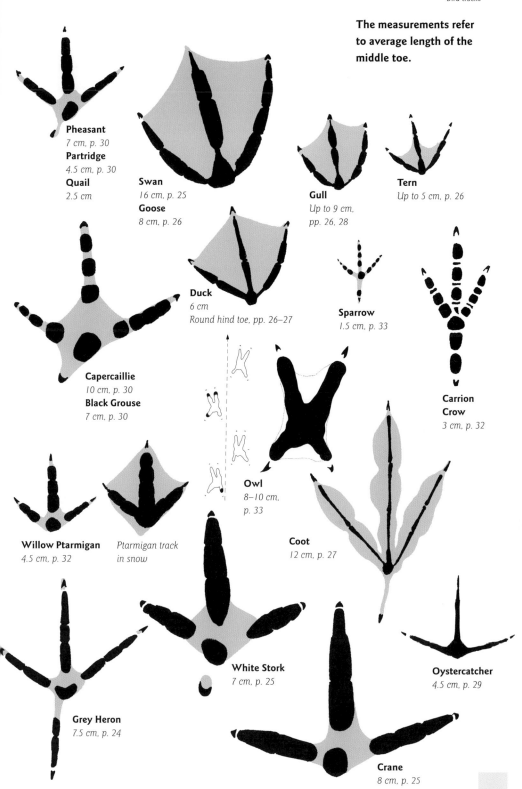

The measurements refer to average length of the middle toe.

Pheasant
7 cm, p. 30
Partridge
4.5 cm, p. 30
Quail
2.5 cm

Swan
16 cm, p. 25
Goose
8 cm, p. 26

Gull
*Up to 9 cm,
pp. 26, 28*

Tern
Up to 5 cm, p. 26

Duck
*6 cm
Round hind toe, pp. 26–27*

Sparrow
1.5 cm, p. 33

Capercaillie
10 cm, p. 30
Black Grouse
7 cm, p. 30

**Carrion
Crow**
3 cm, p. 32

Owl
*8–10 cm,
p. 33*

Willow Ptarmigan
4.5 cm, p. 32

*Ptarmigan track
in snow*

Coot
12 cm, p. 27

Grey Heron
7.5 cm, p. 24

White Stork
7 cm, p. 25

Oystercatcher
4.5 cm, p. 29

Crane
8 cm, p. 25

23

The footprints of herons, bitterns, storks, and cranes are very similar—and all are large.

You can see the tracks of **Grey Herons** on soft ground at the shores of lakes and on the banks of slow-flowing streams or around fishponds. The prints are 15–17 cm long, and the imprint of the middle toe is about 9 cm. In contrast to other wading birds, Grey Heron has a long hind toe which helps it hold onto branches, so Grey Herons are able to build their nests in trees. The hind toe is 6–7 cm long and slightly offset from the front middle toe. The two toes that turn outwards are connected by webbing. Herons have powerful claws, which can be clearly identified in the footprints.

The tracks of **Night Herons** are similar, but 3–6 cm shorter. The toes of **Bitterns** are shorter and slimmer than those of Night Herons.

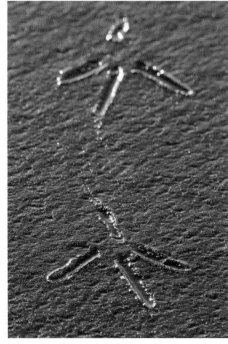

*Frozen tracks of a **Grey Heron** in the ice. AK.*

Grey Heron. *HS.*

Tracks of a **Crane** *in the snow. UR.*

The footprints of cranes show no hind toe. **Cranes** are large and heavy birds, and their footprints can be seen very clearly on soft ground. The inner of the three front toes is shorter than the outer; the print is up to 16 cm in length.

Geese and **swans** are also heavy birds and leave clear footprints. Both species have webbing between the toes. The hind toe is very small; consequently you never see it in a print. Swans' footprints are larger than those of geese, and the prints of both geese and swans are much larger than those of ducks, gulls, and terns.

The footprint of a **swan** is 11–20 cm long. The track of a **Mute Swan** is the largest and may reach 20 cm, though the average is about 16 cm. The track of a **Whooper Swan** measures 14.5 cm on average, that of **Tundra Swan**, 11.5 cm.

Crane. *MH.*

The tracks of **storks** can be found in wet meadows and fields and in the soft mud or sand around ponds and lakes. Since it is a heavy bird, the footprints are usually very clear. The prints of the toes are shorter and broader than those of a heron, about 14–15 cm long. The middle toe is 7–8 cm long. The hind toe is only 2–2.5 cm long and can often only be seen as a small dot in the print.

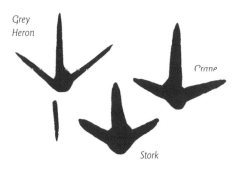

Grey
Heron

Crane

Stork

Comparison of the tracks of a Grey Heron, a stork, and a Crane.

Tracks of **swans** in the mud.

Tracks of a **Mallard** in wet sand. GEH.

Goose footprints are about 6–12 cm long. **Domestic geese** leave the largest tracks; often longer than 12 cm. The footprints of **Greylag Geese** are 10–12 cm long. The prints of other species of goose are shorter and narrower. The footprint of a **Canada Goose** is about 10 cm long, that of a **Bean Goose** about 8 cm, and that of **Brent Goose** about 6 cm.

Ducks, gulls, and **terns** also have webbing between their three front toes, like swans and geese. Ducks normally move with their toes pointed inward, whereas the footprints of gulls are normally pretty much straight or parallel. The prints of a duck's hind toes are often visible, but this is rarely the case with gulls and terns.

Ducks' toes are narrower than those of geese, and the longer and more pointed claws are clearly visible. The duck's stride is shorter than that of a goose. The hind toe of dabbling ducks leaves only a small, narrow print. The hind toe of a diving duck has a spur, and as a result leaves a larger print. The outer toe of diving ducks is longer and more curved than the middle toe. The middle toe of dabbling ducks is the longest. **Mallard** footprints are about 7.5–8 cm long.

Dabbling ducks sit high in the water, and their tails are always above the surface. Diving ducks sit deeper in the water, and their tail dips into the water.

Dabbling ducks go ashore more regularly in search of food, and as a result you see their tracks more often.

Brent Geese. MH.

*Tracks of a **Goose** in the sand.*

Dabbling ducks rarely dive, finding it sufficient to dip their head under the water, at which point their tail sticks up in the air. Diving ducks often dive to the bottom and can stay submerged for a long time. Diving ducks take off directly from the surface of the water, whereas dabbling ducks have to run on the surface before taking off.

The tracks of **Coots** are very distinctive. They have lobes on each of the three front toes. The print is about 12 cm long and about 10 cm wide. The hind toe leaves a small print.

Moorhen has long, small toes and a hind toe that is 1.5 cm long, and which often points inward. The print is about 9.5 cm long and 8 cm wide.

Grebes have restricted webbing between their feet, but do have long, wide lobes on the three front toes. The hind toe print is almost never visible. A **Great Crested Grebe** footprint is about 7.5 cm long and about 6.5 cm wide.

*A **Cormorant** dries its feathers. AK.*

Gulls have webbing that extends up to the claws of the three front toes. The hind toe usually leaves no print. Gulls and terns scurry around, and this is the reason you encounter many overlapping tracks. Ducks

move in a more goal-oriented manner and therefore have a longer stride. The footprint of **Black-headed Gull** is about 4.5 cm long, **Common Gull** about 5 cm, **Lesser Black-backed Gull** 6.5–7 cm, and that of **Herring** and **Great Black-backed Gulls** about 9 cm.

In **terns**, the webbing between the three front toes is more restricted. The footprints are really small, since these are very light birds. The footprints' length is about 3.5–4.5 cm.

A **Cormorant** has webbing between its three front toes, and its hind toe is also connected to the three front ones. The outer toe is longer than the three other toes.

The length of the footprint is up to 13 cm, the width up to 12 cm. Cormorants normally don't go ashore. They mostly stand, relax, and dry their feathers on stumps or other man-made structures away from the shore. Cormorants' footprints are often close together since they hop around a little at take-off. You often find tracks of a number of Cormorants in the same place.

The tracks of waders can be seen on muddy surfaces and on beaches with fine, wet sand. The footprints of the large **Curlew**

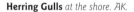

Herring Gulls *at the shore. AK.*

Little Stints *and* **Dunlin** *look for food. HS.*

are about 5.5 cm long, those of **Woodcocks** and **Oystercatchers** about 4.5 cm, those of **Ruff** about 4 cm, those of **Lapwings**, **Snipe**, and **plovers** are all about 3.5 cm. The footprints of **Dunlin**, **Common Ringed Plover**, **Sanderling**, and **Ruddy Turnstone** are 3 cm in length or less.

You will often find small holes in the immediate vicinity of wader footprints; this is where birds have poked their beaks into the sand searching for crustaceans, worms, and other food. Occasionally you may also find the remains of a bird's meal as well as the bird's droppings.

Capercaillie is a large, heavy bird with strong legs; its tracks can be found on soft ground in woodland and forest. Its claws are long and leave clear prints. The hind toe is small, only about 2.5–3 cm long, but it leaves a clear impression. The three

Footprints of **Redshanks** *and* **Greenshanks** *on the mudflats, with marks made by their probing beaks. AC.*

front toes are longer. The male's foot-print is about 8–12 cm long and 7–11 cm wide. In winter you can see the prints of stiff, brush-like fur between the bird's toes. The female's footprint is only about two-thirds the size of the male's. You can find the prints best in winter, usually between trees in coniferous forest.

The tracks of **Black Grouse** resemble those of Capercaillie, but they are smaller, 7–8 cm long and 6–7 cm wide; the prints can usually be found at woodland edges, on moorland or heathland, or at lake shores, wherever grouse have their leks.

The **Pheasant** is a relatively heavy bird with strong legs. As is the case with other game birds, the toes have powerful claws which are used to dig in the earth. The hind toe print is very small and positioned obliquely inward relative to the front mid-dle toe. The hind toe print is just 1–2 cm long. The footprint is 6.5–7.5 cm long and 6–6.5 cm wide. Pheasants walk or run, and this explains why you only rarely see paired prints.

Partridge tracks are similar to those of Pheasants, but are only 4.5 cm long. They are less frequently found in sum-mer, but when birds gather in small groups

Lapwing. MH.

Capercaillie (male). BG.

A **Capercaillie** track. EH.

in winter, you can find prints as deep rows running in a straight line.

Lapwings leave tracks on sandy soil and other soft terrain. The hind toe leaves no print since it is situated fairly high up. A Lapwing's toes are spaced well apart; the footprint is 3.5–4 cm long and slightly broader than it is long.

A **Lapwing** track.

Black Grouse. *BG.*

Grey Partridge. *SS.*

Black Grouse *track. UR.*

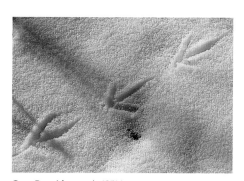

Grey Partridge *track. JORN.*

Grey Partridge. *HBH.*

Willow Ptarmigan *in winter plumage. AK.*

sequence may be seen as a winding band, especially when fresh in snow.

Crows and jays have a hind toe that is almost exactly as long as the front middle toe. The footprint is really narrow, and all toes are equipped with long claws. The footprints of **Carrion Crows** are about 6.5 cm long and 3.5 cm wide; the hind toe is about 2.5 cm long. Crows often move by hopping; that is why the prints are seen together, in pairs.

You will regularly find **Magpie** tracks, since the birds are common in urban areas. The print is about 5 cm long and 3 cm wide; the toes are 'calloused' on the underside, and occasionally prints of the callouses are visible.

Pigeons have relatively powerful legs with which they can hold onto branches the way crows and jays do, but their claws are not as long, and their footprints are somewhat shorter and wider. The

Footprint of a **Carrion Crow**. *JJ.*

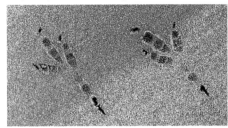

Willow Ptarmigan *tracks in an upland birch wood. AK.*

Willow Ptarmigan have toes covered with feathers, and this means their footprints are somewhat blurred. The overall track is 4.5 cm long, and the track

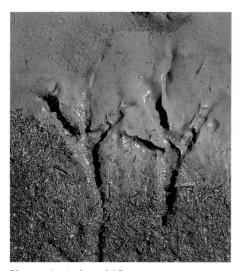

Pigeon *prints in the mud. LG.*

Footprint of a **Meadow Pipit**. *LG.*

footprint of the **Wood Pigeon** is about 6 cm long and 5 cm wide; the hind toe is longer than that of any game-bird species and shorter than that of crows and jays. It is placed at an angle to the middle toe.

Occasionally, on soft ground, you can find the tracks of a male dove that has circled a female during courtship.

The tracks of **small birds** are almost un-identifiable. Most of these passerines have a long hind toe, so they can hold onto the branches of bushes and trees. Birds often hop, but some walk. A **Blackbird's** tracks are 5.5 cm long and 3 cm wide, those of sparrows 2.5–3 cm long and about 1.5 cm wide.

Owl prints are easily recognised, since the birds have two front and two hind toes, and the tracks are very large and clear. You will frequently see claw marks. The footprint of an **Eagle Owl**, not including the claws, measures about 10.5 cm.

A **Hawk Owl** *has caught a mouse in the snow. MV.*

Hawk Owl. *HS.*

33

Tracks of a **Willow Ptarmigan** *taking off. AK.*

Scat

Scat is normally clear and easily seen as the sign of the presence of a mammal, and it is widespread in the wild. Compared with other more subtle signs, scat is often distinctive and easy to attribute to a particular species. You will discover a great deal about an animal's diet by analysing scat, as well as information about its behaviour and the habitats in which it lives.

Carnivores

Meat is protein rich and can be digested pretty efficiently by carnivores. This is why carnivores leave behind less copious amounts of scat than do herbivores, and why the scat is usually more solid. Carnivore scat is normally cylindrical, and one end is often pointed. Based on shape, colour, size, and content, you can often identify the scat of individual species. Scat can contain significant quantities of hair,

feathers, teeth, and bone from the animals that were consumed; thus you may also be able to determine the prey species eaten by the carnivore.

However, it is not always true that the animals whose remains you find in the scat were killed by the carnivore, since most carnivores are opportunistic and will also consume carrion.

Many carnivores use their scat as a way to mark territory, a clear sign to members of their own and sometimes other species, and the scat may be left in a conspicuous place for this very reason; the scat is often pungent, too.

Many carnivores will also eat plants, especially fruit and berries in summer and autumn, and when they do, their scat may be softer and generally more shapeless.

Carnivore scat may be confused with owl pellets (*cf.* p. 83), but carnivore scat is usually segmented and often twisted. Hairs lie lengthwise in carnivore scat, and it is almost always pointed at one end.

Brown Bear. *AK*.

Carnivore scat

Approx. one-half actual size

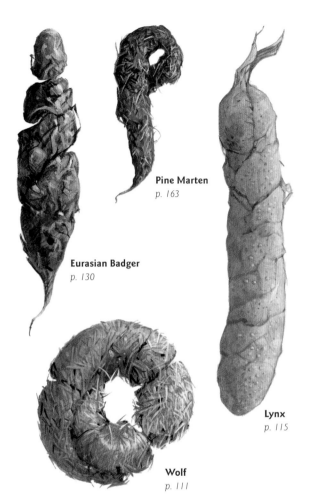

Pine Marten
p. 163

Eurasian Badger
p. 130

Cat *scat. L-HO.*

Wolf
p. 111

Lynx
p. 115

Brown Bear
p. 106

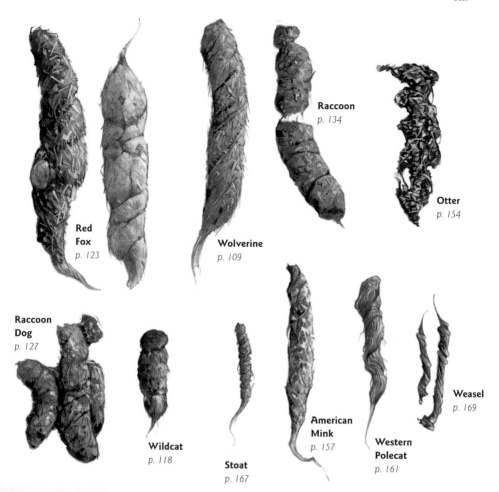

Red Fox
p. 123

Wolverine
p. 109

Raccoon
p. 134

Otter
p. 154

Raccoon Dog
p. 127

Wildcat
p. 118

Stoat
p. 167

American Mink
p. 157

Western Polecat
p. 161

Weasel
p. 169

A **Red Fox** *defecating. LG.*

Scat of smaller mammals

Approx. actual size

Norway Lemming
p. 216

Bat
p. 229

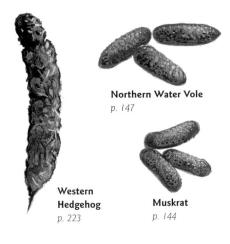

Northern Water Vole
p. 147

House Mouse
p. 192

Wood Mouse
p. 199

Western Hedgehog
p. 223

Muskrat
p. 144

Common Vole
p. 213

Harvest Mouse
p. 202

Yellow-necked Mouse
p. 195

Water Shrew
p. 151

Scat of larger rodents

Approx. actual size

Flying Squirrel
p. 184

Red Squirrel
p. 179

Rabbit
p. 176

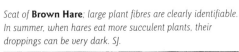

Brown Hare
p. 171

Black Rat
p. 188

*Scat of **Brown Hare**; large plant fibres are clearly identifiable. In summer, when hares eat more succulent plants, their droppings can be very dark. SJ.*

Coypu
p. 143

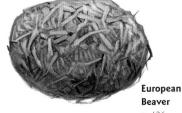

European Beaver
p. 136

Bat *scat on a roof beam, one of the few visible signs these animals leave behind. PB.*

Roving **rats** *live anywhere they can find food. Here a rat has found a shelter with bird food. It has dug through two wheelbarrow loads of gravel under the tiles and left signs of its activity in the form of loose tiles as well as scat. AK.*

Bat *scat. LG.*

Rat *tail tracks in flour. PW.*

Roe Deer *scat. LG.*

Scat of larger herbivores

Compared with a carnivore's diet, a herbivore's diet is poor in nutrients; this is why herbivores must consume more food and therefore produce greater quantities of scat than carnivores do. Herbivore scat is often left in lumps. The scat is mostly small and round and contains the ground-up remains of plants. In summer, when the plants are succulent, the scat may contain a lot of water, and it can also be larger and looser in consistency, taking on the appearance of a cowpat.

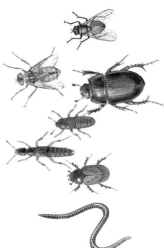

Cowpats *attract many small animals, mostly flies, earthworms, and beetles. AK. p. 232*

Horse
p. 231

Approx. one-third actual size

Wild Boar
p. 233

Old **horse** *scat. AK.*

A young **Wild Boar**. *SS.*

Elk *leave scat in a cohesive lump. In summer the scat is very soft and dark. Depending on its diet, an Elk's scat may look like a cowpat. In winter it is harder in consistency and lighter in colour, and will also contain larger plant fibres. AK.*

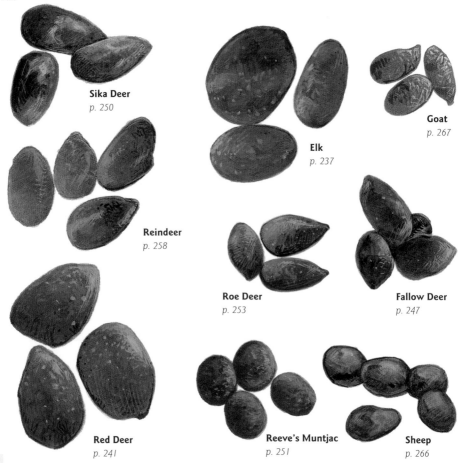

Sika Deer
p. 250

Goat
p. 267

Elk
p. 237

Reindeer
p. 258

Roe Deer
p. 253

Fallow Deer
p. 247

Red Deer
p. 241

Reeve's Muntjac
p. 251

Sheep
p. 266

Bird droppings

Birds excrete urine in the form of a small white or grey spot at one end of the dropping. It's not possible to distinguish the droppings of small bird species from one another, but many larger birds leave characteristic droppings.

Swans, geese, and ducks are plant eaters, and you will often come across their long, rounded droppings in large quantities along the shores of lakes, rivers, and streams and in meadows. The droppings comprise compacted plant matter.

Swan droppings are up to 15 cm long and 2 cm thick. When fresh, they are green but gradually become grey over time.

Goose droppings are 5–8 cm long and 10–12 mm thick; the droppings of **ducks** are about 4 cm long.

The droppings of **game birds** are slightly curved and normally yellow-brown to dark brown. They can be found individually or in quantity below the birds' roost sites. Game bird droppings may be confused with those of hedgehogs, which will, however, always contain insect remains. See p. 38.

The droppings of the **Capercaillie** are yellow-green, about 10 cm. long and 1.2 cm thick, and they later turn to a greyish brown. In the winter they comprise almost exclusively the remains of fir needles. One can find them in quantity beneath the trees used by the Capercaillies as a roost site.

Willow Ptarmigan droppings. AK.

Hazel Grouse droppings. SJ.

The droppings of **Black Grouse** are about 5 cm long; when fresh they are greenish or light yellow, later they become a greyish brown, and you find them mostly near the birds' leks.

The droppings of **Hazel Grouse** and **Willow Ptarmigan** are 6–7 cm long and 1.5–2 cm thick; they are very compact and may be found scattered in upland areas where these birds live.

In winter, **Capercaillie** *droppings comprise almost exclusively the remains of fir needles. ED.*

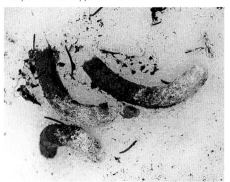

Black Grouse droppings. HN.

Approx. one-third actual size

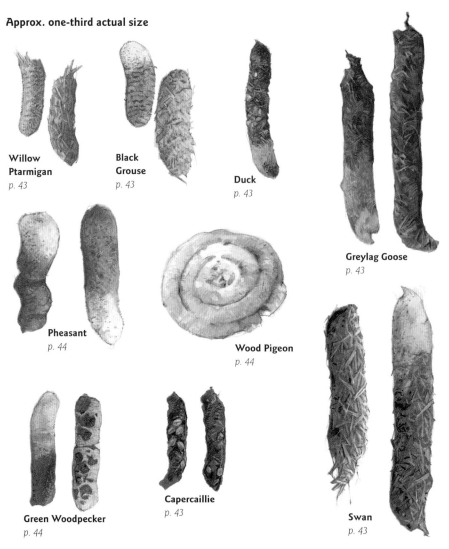

Willow
Ptarmigan
p. 43

Black
Grouse
p. 43

Duck
p. 43

Greylag Goose
p. 43

Pheasant
p. 44

Wood Pigeon
p. 44

Green Woodpecker
p. 44

Capercaillie
p. 43

Swan
p. 43

Pheasant droppings are about 2 cm long and 4–5 mm thick and usually white at one end as a result of colouration by urine. In summer they can be somewhat more fluid, but most of the year they are more solid and blackish brown or greenish.

With insectivores you can find and identify the remains of insects the birds have eaten.

Green Woodpecker droppings are en-closed in an ash-grey skin and may contain the remains of undigested parts of ants.

Some birds in summer and autumn feed mainly on fruit and berries, and the droppings are coloured by this diet and may also contain stones and kernels, for example, **Blackbirds** and other thrushes.

Many birds have regular roost sites in trees, and beneath these you will find large quantities of droppings, for example, birds such as **Wood Pigeon**, whose long and twisted droppings are somewhat reminiscent of worm casts.

The nest sites of colonial nesting birds are whitewashed by droppings, as you can see on cliffs used by seabirds. **Eagle** and **owl** nests are also filled with droppings.

Cormorants can whitewash nesting areas with their droppings; the trees in which the birds nest may actually die from the abnormal absorption of nutrients.

Grey Herons breed in colonies in trees. Their droppings are found mostly under the trees in which they are nesting or on the edges of lakes, rivers, and streams. The droppings are 4.5–8 cm long and 2.5–4 mm thick and contain hair and feathers as well as occasionally the remains of bones of small mammals.

Young **terns**, **seagulls**, and **Cormorants** can stain rocks white with their droppings. AK.

Cormorant droppings corrode the leaves of the trees in which the birds nest; the trees become completely white and may eventually die. LG.

Feeding signs on trees

The bark, branches, and especially shoots of mostly young trees and bushes play an important role as food for many animals in winter. This is true for deer, goats, hares, as well as many small rodents and squirrels.

In most cases, tooth marks will be clearly recognisable in the bark; depending on the size and appearance of the individual tooth marks, you may be able to identify the animal responsible.

A rutting **Red Deer**. *LG.*

Red Deer *gnaw marks on a pine tree, with peeled-off bark and resin. SS.*

Elk *gnaw marks on a young oak. ÅK.*

In winter, **Elk** *eat lots of pine needles. MOF.*

The result of **deer** *grazing on a young spruce. SS.*

Mouflon *tracks around a young oak. PB.*

Mouflon *with young. Biopix.*

Field Vole
A stump worked on by a Field Vole; the marks of the front teeth are visible here. PB.
Upper right: Raspberry shoots cut down by Field Voles. PB.
Middle: A chewed-off spruce branch. PB.

Bank Vole
Lower right: Douglas fir with the feeding signs of a Bank Vole on the bark. PB.
Below: Tooth marks on the uppermost buds of a white fir. PB.

European Beaver

The powerful front teeth of the **European Beaver**, especially in its protruding lower jaw, are perfectly designed for tackling trees.

European Beavers have small ears, thick whiskers, and webbing between their toes. DW.

European Beavers need water and access to building materials. LGA.

A large birch felled by a **European Beaver,** *resulting in the typical cone-shaped stump. LGA.*

Occasionally **European Beavers** *peel trees without felling them; in this case a Scotch pine. PB.*

A partially peeled birch trunk with noticeable tooth marks. PB.

*Young **bears** playing. LG.*

*The trunk of a pine tree with visible **bear** scratches. EM.*

*The **Wolverine** has very sharp claws on its front legs and readily scratches bark. ME.*

Northern Water Vole. *Above: Tooth marks at the root of an apple tree in winter. The whole root may be eaten, and consequently the tree can easily fall. PB. Right: Tooth marks on an ash in summer; at the foot of the tree, chewed-off bits of bark. PB. Below, a Northern Water Vole. WP.*

*A **Wild Boar** roots around on the forest floor. Biopix. Inset: After a **Wild Boar** has wallowed, it often rubs off the mud on large trees.*

A **Red Squirrel** *has chewed off beech branches to get to the buds. PB.*

Red Squirrel *tooth marks left while searching for bark beetle larvae hiding in the round holes. PB.*

A branch criss-crossed by **Brown Hare** *tooth marks. Below left:* **Hares** *feeding on fruit trees can cause the trees to die. PB.*

The ears of a **Brown Hare** *are larger than those of a Rabbit. LG.*

Gnaw marks of a **Mountain Hare** *on branches show as clean cuts, and are not frayed like those of deer. AK.*

Brown Hares *can gnaw the bark from small branches, particularly in winter. LAD.*

Mountain *and* **Brown Hare** *are very similar species (cf. p. 174). AK.*

Rabbits *readily gnaw the bark of branches, here a pine tree. AK.*

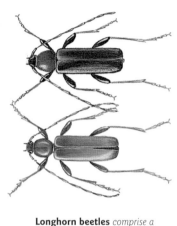

Longhorn beetles *comprise a group of medium-sized beetles; here a tanbark borer. The larvae live between the bark and the wood at the core of living and dead trees; they excavate a clearly visible system of tunnels. You can find the adult beetles on flowers.*

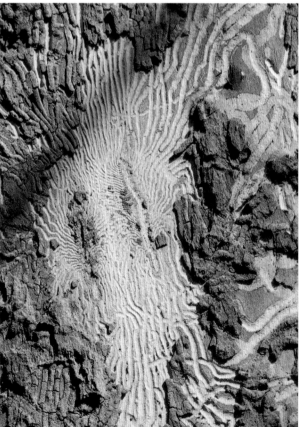

Bark beetles *are a group of very small beetles that breed between the bark and the core wood of various deciduous and evergreen trees (below: ash bark beetle, bark beetle, and a European shothole borer). Every species has its own tunnel pattern. AK.*

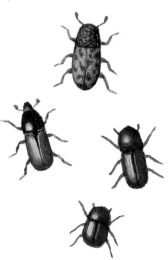

Fray marks on trees

*In the spring, **Roe Deer** shed the velvet on their antlers by rubbing the antlers on small trees and bushes. The rub marks are also used as territorial signals. SDL.*

Red Deer *have rubbed the trunk of this spruce.*

Red Deer *antler rubbing in a spruce clearing. LS.*

With deer, fraying of bark is caused by deer rubbing their antlers to remove the velvet. It is most frequently found only on one side of a tree and leaves strips of bark hanging from the trunk. A more aggressive type of rubbing occurs during rutting. At this time males often simulate combat to relieve aggression, using trees as substitutes for real opponents. When they do this, damage to a tree is significantly more extensive and may include completely stripping the bark around the trunk, breaking branches, and making some deeper gashes on the trunk. These various marks also serve as territorial markers.

*With **Red Deer**, rubbing to remove the velvet occurs from July to August, while rubbing during the rutting season takes place from September to October.*

Holes in trees, ant heaps, etc.

Woodpeckers excavate holes for their nests. The entrance hole is round and often high up on a trunk. Woodpeckers make a new nest hole every year; the old one is used by many other creatures, including small mammals.

Woodpeckers are equipped with two hind and two foretoes, allowing them to maintain a firm grip on the bark of trunks and branches, and they can then move up and down looking for insects, larvae, and pupae. You find these holes especially in weakened, old, or dead trees, where the bark is falling off—so-called **woodpecker trees**. You can also see traces of the chisel-shaped beaks of woodpeckers, and at the foot of the tree there are often large piles of wood shavings.

When a **Black Woodpecker** excavates its way into the nest of black wood ants or black Ross ants, the resulting holes may be large. **Black, White-backed,** and **Green Woodpeckers** assiduously search in old tree trunks for insects. They can transform a stump into a pile of wood shavings in no time at all.

A **Black Woodpecker** *feeding young.* LG.

Characteristic peck marks of a **Three-toed Woodpecker** *on a pine.* AK.

A male **Three-toed Woodpecker**. *THLU.*

Woodpeckers *can also excavate holes in the gables of wooden houses, or in nest boxes (here a Swift box), so they can get at the eggs or young of small birds. L-HO.*

Small holes in trees are created by a variety of insects with larvae living in the dead trunks beneath the bark: **wood wasps**, **bark beetles**, *and* **fiery clearwings**.
Inset: Hind part of the body of a **cardinal beetle**. *AK.*

Shavings on the ground are the result of a **woodpecker***'s work on a tree trunk. AK.*

Large holes in ant nests are often the result of **Green** *or* **Black Woodpeckers** *hunting for ants. The holes are visible only when the ants aren't active outside the nest. L-HO.*

Wood ants, **Ross ants**, and **termites** *make nests in trees; they can eat through trunks to such an extent that the trunks end up looking like dried-out sponges.*

Some **titmice** *excavate holes for their nests in dead tree trunks, stumps, or weak live trees, but the holes are not as high up as those excavated by woodpeckers.*

Brown Bears *love wood ants; they can break off the top of an ants' nest and then root through it. UR.*

Gnawed branches

Red Squirrels *love the male flowers of fir trees; they also eat pineapple galls. The young shoots of pines may lie in heaps at the foot of trees after a squirrel has fed. PB.*

Brown Hares *and* **Rabbits** *have sharp teeth in both their upper and lower jaws; this is why these branches are sheared off (cf. also photo on p. 55). PB.*

Red Squirrels *hold food with their front paws. AK.*

Deer *have no front teeth in their upper jaw and must twist off branches; this is the reason deer-grazed branches have frayed tips. AK.*

Northern Water Voles *and* **Field Mice** *use special feeding sites where they feel safe. You usually come across these when the snow melts in spring. The feeding sites can also be in places the animals wouldn't use without adequate snow cover. Gnaw marks and scat reveal which animals have used a particular site. PB.*

Striped Field Mice *like to eat common rushes. The remains may lie like little white sticks alongside the grazed stalks, since only the green part of the plant is eaten.* **Deer** *also feed on common rushes, but they tend to chew off the tips (below). PB.*

Feeding signs on mushrooms

Many animals happily eat mushrooms, especially large boletus. You can often find tooth marks in the flesh of the mushroom.

*Hollow stems and a red secretion on chanterelle are traces of **wireworm larvae**. L-HO.*

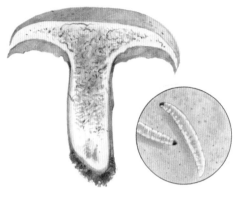

*These small holes in the mushroom are made by the **mushroom gnat**, whose larvae live in the mushroom.*

*A mushroom with the tooth marks of a **mouse**.*

*On the underside of a mushroom, you can find cavities caused by feeding **slugs**.*

Red Squirrels, smaller mammals, **Rabbits**, and **deer** also eat mushrooms. The bite marks may be difficult to identify because of the softness of the mushrooms.

*A **Spanish slug** on a mushroom. AK.*

Feeding signs on turnips

Red Deer pull young turnips from the ground. The animals bite off a piece and leave the rest. When the turnips are ripe, the deer chew on the parts above ground, taking only a little piece from each turnip. The marks of the large lower front teeth show as a wide groove. Small mammals, especially **voles**, feed on turnips, and their teeth marks are very small compared with those of other animals. **Wild Boar** also eat turnips; their teeth marks are clearly visible.

*The teeth of most deer species are smaller than those of **Red Deer**; apart from that, the gnaw marks are similar in appearance.*

Rabbits, like deer, eat only part of the turnip. A Rabbit's upper teeth have a groove, so the feeding marks look like the work of an animal with four small upper teeth and two large lower teeth.

Rats gnaw from above and eat into the turnip, and as a result the tip falls off, and the turnip becomes a hollow husk.

*Gnawed turnips: by **Northern Water Voles** chewing from the bottom (left), by **Rabbits** (middle), and **Red Deer** (right). PB*

Feeding signs on spruce cones

Cones on which squirrels have fed look considerably frayed; the base is long and very frayed; moreover, the tip is not as extensively damaged as when mice feed.

Most of the chewed cones found on the ground in woodland have been eaten by squirrels. When a **squirrel** bites off the cones in a tree, they fall to the ground, where the squirrel then gathers them. It eats them on a stone or a stump from which it can monitor the surroundings, and this is where you will find cones lying in heaps.

*A **squirrel** feeding site with chewed cones. LG.*

*Above: A nut kernel fed on by a **mouse**. Above left and right: Pine cones fed on by **squirrels**. In the middle, a ripe undamaged cone.*

Spruce cones on which **mice** have fed lack the tip of the base, and the other end of the cone also appears rounded. Mice chew in tight rows, giving the cones an even surface in the process. The cone tip is gnawed further up. Mice feed secretively on cones, in places where they feel safe from predators, and this is the reason the cones they've eaten are less easy to find than those consumed by squirrels.

Common Crossbill has a compact but very powerful beak. The upper and lower mandibles are significantly elongated and twisted, and they cross over at the tips. Crossbills split cone scales lengthwise. The cones look frayed but are not as irregular-looking as cones that have been chewed by woodpeckers.

Woodpeckers hack and pry the scales apart in order to reach the seeds, and this is why cones look frayed, with twisted and

*A **Common Crossbill** at a spruce cone. SS.*

Left: *A spruce cone with scales split by a **Common Crossbill**; right: pecked at by a **woodpecker**.*

*The workshop of a **Great Spotted Woodpecker** on an old stump. TH.*

broken scales that stick out in all directions. Woodpeckers stick cones in the cracks of trees such as hazels. The cones often lie in great numbers under a woodpecker's workshop, or you can find them stuck in the bark or cracks in the trunk of a tree.

67

*A **Parrot Crossbill** with a pine cone. LG.*

*A **Striped Field Mouse** with a hazelnut. LG.*

Feeding signs on pine cones

*Pine cones on which **squirrels** have fed are considerably frayed and show numerous scales at the tip.*

*Cones fed on by **mice** (left) show marks that are close together, and the cones have fewer scales at the tip. (Right) **Woodpeckers** are less methodical when feeding on pine cones, and this gives the cone an irregularly frayed appearance.*

Feeding signs on hazelnuts

In all mammals only the lower jaw is mobile, and rodents can gnaw only with the teeth in their lower jaw. Mice work on hazelnuts in two ways.

*Voles, such as **Bank Vole**, and **Striped Field Mouse** stick the upper front teeth into the shell and gnaw at the hole with their bottom incisors to make it larger, working from the outside towards the centre, so you see no marks of the upper teeth on the outside of the shell.*

*True mice such as **Wood Mouse**, **Yellow-necked Mouse**, and **Northern Water Vole** stick the lower teeth into the shell and gnaw an increasingly larger hole on the opposite side of the nut, from the inside out, while holding the nut with the upper teeth, turning the nut as they do so. The upper teeth leave noticeable marks on the outside of the hole just below the edge. Here we see the tooth marks of a **Yellow-necked Mouse**. LG.*

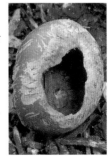

Squirrels *chew at the shell, then use the teeth in their lower jaw like a jimmy. Older squirrels, with stronger teeth and more experience, leave only a few tooth marks, younger ones more.*

Green hazelnuts with signs of **squirrel** *feeding.*

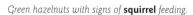

 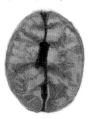

Hazelnut with signs of feeding by a **Great Tit**. *The beak marks of Great Tits are very small, and the birds prefer nuts that have not fully ripened, when the shell is still soft.*

The beak of a **woodpecker** *is flattened at the tip; for this reason the marks on nuts run vertically. Beak marks of a* **Great Spotted Woodpecker** *are about 2 mm long. Woodpeckers wedge nuts in crevices of trees so they can peck at them, or they make a hole in a tree in which they fit the nut. At the foot of the tree, you can find many split nuts; this is what is called a woodpecker's 'workshop'. KS.*

Hazelnut with the signs of feeding by a **woodpecker**. *Left, with peck marks; on the right, an emptied nut.*

*The tips of the beaks of **Jay** and **Magpie** are sharply pointed, and, as with nuthatches, only the tip of the beak leaves a mark on the shell of a nut. SS.*

Nutcracker *in a pine, MH.*

*The upper mandible of a **Nuthatch** protrudes slightly over the lower, and this is the reason the beak marks resemble a half-moon. The birds lodge the nut in a natural crevice in the tree, where it often remains permanently stuck, reducing the accumulation of empty shells. GH.*

Nutcrackers *cache provisions for winter in the ground. They hold a nut with one foot and often peck at its tip. Their pecking is so powerful that the shell is split in two. They work on nuts at special feeding sites, for instance on a stump or a moss-covered stone.*

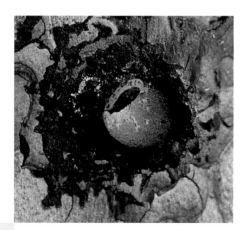

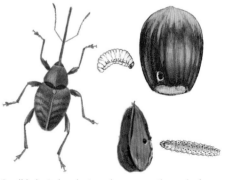

Small holes in hazelnuts and acorns are the work of **hazelnut weevils***; small holes in beechnuts are the work of* **leafroller larvae***.*

Feeding signs on walnuts

Mice *leave an even round hole in the shell with noticeable tooth marks*

Crossbills *eat only walnuts with thin shells; they bite the shell along the seam, splitting the nut in two.*

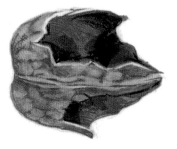

Great Tits *can peck through only the thin spots in a shell; as a result the holes they leave are less regular.*

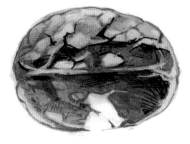

Red Squirrels *do not gnaw on walnuts; instead, they press their lower teeth into a thin spot in the shell and open the nut by twisting it; this is why you will find no tooth marks on nuts they have opened.*

Jackdaws *prefer gathering walnuts directly from the tree and then flying to a feeding site, where they peck large, irregular holes with their powerful beaks.*

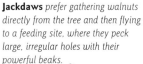

Red Squirrel *with a walnut. AK.*

Thrushes

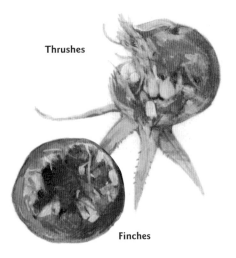

Finches

Greenfinch *on a rose hip. BW.*

Feeding signs on rose hips

Red Squirrels readily eat rose hips. Since they cannot sit on the flimsy branches of rose bushes, they eat the rose hips on the ground, biting them lengthwise to reach the core. **Mice** gnaw sideways into the rose hip and pull the core out, leaving the remains lying under the bushes at feeding sites. Mice are secretive when feeding, so the remains of a meal are usually hidden.

Numerous birds, like **Fieldfare** and other thrushes, eat the red flesh of the fruit and leave the core behind. **Finches**—Greenfinch, for instance—peck into the flesh of the fruit just to reach the seeds; they do not eat the flesh itself.

Rose hips with **Greenfinch** *feeding signs. BB.*

Rose hips with **Red Squirrel** *feeding signs (left and middle);* **mice** *(right).*

Feeding signs on cherry stones

Starlings and **thrushes** do not eat cherry stones, only the fruit itself. The unchewed stones may stay attached to the stem, or lie in heaps at the foot of the tree.

A **Fieldfare** eating cherries. AK.

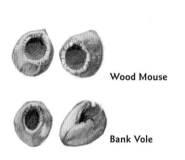

Wood Mouse

Bank Vole

Mice routinely chew holes in cherry stones to reach the soft contents; they gnaw holes in the stones the same way they do in hazelnuts.

Cherry stone with **Bank Vole** feeding signs. AK.

Hawfinch. MH.

Hawfinches do not eat the flesh of the fruit, but instead empty the stone after cracking it with their powerful beak. They split the stones in two, leaving no beak marks on the shell. You can find many split cherry stones under a tree. Hawfinches handle the stones of a range of fruit trees in the same fashion.

Feeding signs on apples

Many mammals love apples. **Roe Deer** and **Wild Boar** will actually break into gardens to eat fallen fruit, whereas **Red Deer** and **Elk** pluck the fruit directly from trees. Normally they don't leave a morsel behind, but they do leave tracks.

Some small animals, like **Bank Voles** and **dormice**, can gnaw apples hanging on the tree, but most rodents only eat and gnaw at fallen or ripe fruit. It can be difficult to determine which species has fed on the fruit. The size of the tooth marks gives only a hint as to whether it was an animal the size of a mouse or rather an animal with teeth that are twice the size, like squirrels, rats, or Northern Water Vole.

Field Vole. *LG.*

Birds, especially **Blackbirds** and other **thrushes**, love apples. They sometimes peck at apples while they still hang on the trees; however, most birds peck and feed on them once they have fallen to the ground. They hollow the apples into a bowl shape, but do not consume the core.

Wasps also relish sweet fruit in autumn. They can also hollow out apples and leave only a small hole in the peel. Naturnettet.dk.

Parrot Crossbills dig into the apples to reach the core; they prefer smaller cultivated apple varieties and other wild apples, since these have a lot of core and relatively little flesh.

Worms in apples. Small holes in apples and other fruit are the work of the larvae of the **small (apple) codling moth**.

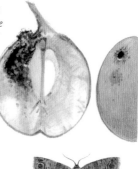

Redwing on an apple. HS.

Nests and dens

In constructing their dens, all animals try to camouflage or obscure them as best they can. Nests and dens are often hard to see, but they can sometimes be found if you follow an animal's tracks.

Brown Hares *prepare what is called a 'form', a depression in high grass, or often under a large stone, among other places. When a hare is in its form, it is almost impossible to see. Left, LG; right, AT.*

Brown Bears *hibernate in a den excavated in a mound of earth, between rocks, or under an old ants' nest. Left, AK; right, RA.*

A **Rabbit** burrow in a sandy hill with a latrine. Left, PB; right, SS.

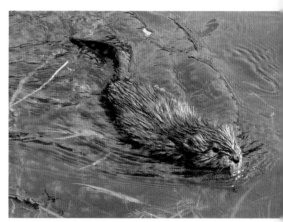

A **Muskrat** burrow near a frozen lake; the entrance hole is under the ice. Left, PB; right, SOJ.

The dens of **Eurasian Badger** resemble those of foxes, but they can be larger, and the excavated material will be carried further away. In front of the burrow you find a distinct rut where the animal has dragged nesting material into the den. Left, PB; right, LG.

*The entrance to a **molehill** is usually in the middle of the mound. Left, PB; right, LG.*

*The entrance hole for the **Northern Water Vole** is next to its mound. Left, PB; right, LG.*

*An entrance hole for a **rat**, with a well-trampled and compacted runway. PB.*

*The system of passageways created by a **Wood Mouse** reaches about a metre underground. SS.*

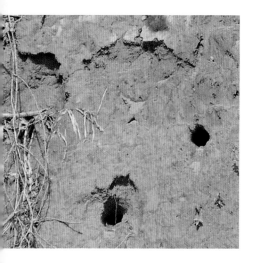

Kingfishers *dig long tunnels on steep slopes, especially near slow-flowing water or lakes. There are separate entrance holes to the nest. LG.*

Bee-eaters *dig holes in banks by lakes, gravel pits, etc., and usually in colonies. HS.*

Sand Martins *dig long straight passageways in sandy banks, especially near water. The holes are often high up, and they are always grouped together. Left, MH; right, LG.*

Small holes, especially in sandy soil or gravel paths, are made by **spider wasps** or **mammoth wasps**, which dig passage-ways for their larvae. Around the holes you will see excavated material in the form of cones or strips. Left, HO; right, SDL.

Small round holes, with a diameter of about 10 cm, especially in dry sandy soil, are made by small birds which have taken a sand bath to clean their feathers and rid them-selves of small parasites. LG.

Honey Buzzards and **Eurasian Badgers** can excavate the ground nests of wasps and bumblebees to reach the insects. Eurasian Badger hunts for bumblebees more thoroughly than Honey Buzzards do. The badgers eat almost everything, while the Honey Buzzards leave considerable portions of the nest behind. RJS; inset, KH.

The telltale sign of a **Eurasian Badger**'s *snout: it's been digging for earthworms. LG.*

You only rarely see **earthworm** *holes in the summer, but in autumn, winter, and spring, leaves and other plant remains are more visible near worm holes, where the worms have dragged food into their tunnels. Worm casts lie scattered on the ground in small heaps and are similar to the casts of sandworms on a beach at low tide. PN.*

Black garden ants *dig their nests in loose sandy soil; the excavated soil lies in small sand hills around the entrance holes. PN.*

Ant highway: **wood ants** *use clearly visible trails that run to the nests. AK.*

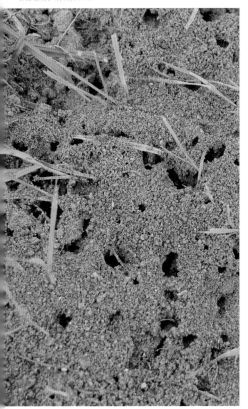

Pellets

Owls, raptors, crows and jays, storks, herons, gulls, nightjars, bee-eaters, kingfishers, and many small birds expel indigestible parts of their food. The pellets are often found at the birds' favoured perches and lookouts, and close to their nests. Most species produce a single pellet twice a day.

Pellets are normally drier than the scat of mammals, often rounded at both ends, and contain hair, feathers, insect remains, and parts of skulls and skeletons. If you're lucky, you can also find undigested rings from ringed birds in them as well.

Sometimes it is difficult to determine whether something is a bird's pellet or mammal scat, and in this case only shape, content, and location will help identification.

Pellet of a **Short-eared Owl**. *AK.*

Identification of specific bird species from pellets can be even more difficult, but again, shape, content, and location can offer significant clues.

Owl pellets

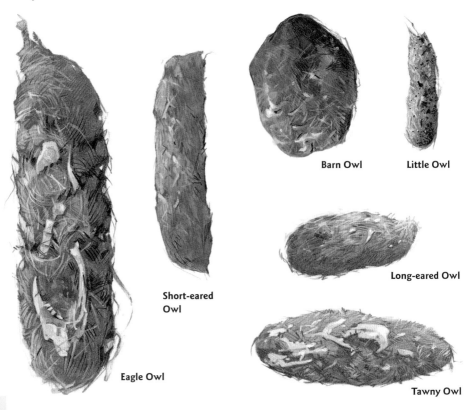

Barn Owl

Little Owl

Short-eared Owl

Long-eared Owl

Eagle Owl

Tawny Owl

Owl pellets

Owl pellets are normally grey and usually consist of tightly compacted remains of bones, insects, and feathers. Inside a pellet, hairs lie in every direction; pellets are never twisted, and they are usually not pointed. Occasionally pellets will contain the entire skull of a small mammal, and you will often find many pellets in the same place.

The pellets of **Tawny Owls** are 4–6 cm long and 2–3 cm wide, normally slightly pointed at one or both ends, and usually have a rough surface. They always contain clearly identifiable bones and often entire skulls of mice, Northern Water Voles, shrews, and the remains of insects as well. They can be found near nests and at favoured perches in woodland. The perch is normally close to the trunk of a fir tree.

The pellets of **Long-eared Owls** are somewhat narrower than those of Tawny Owls: 4–8 cm long, but no wider than 2.5 cm, normally rounded at both ends, and with a smooth surface. They almost always contain the remains of mice. Owls often gather in small groups in winter, and this is why you will sometimes find many pellets in a small area.

Short-eared Owl pellets are similar to those of Long-eared Owl, but may be a little longer. They consist almost exclusively of the hair and bones of Common Voles, and can be found under the birds' nests, on mounds in fields and meadows, and above the treeline in more mountainous areas.

The pellets of **Barn Owls** are wrapped in a black, shiny-slick slime when fresh. They are about 3–8 cm long, about 3 cm wide, and rounded at both ends. They are almost always found in barns or abandoned buildings in rural areas, where the owls have their nests or roosts.

The pellets of **Little Owls** are small, 2–5 cm long and about 1.5 cm wide, often rounded at one end, and pointed at the other. In summer, Little Owls feed mostly on insects; at this time the bulk of the pellets comprise insect remains but may also contain earth from digested earthworms as well as feathers of small birds. In winter, the pellets you find usually contain the remains of mice and small birds. The pellets are usually near hollow trees or in buildings where the owls nest or roost during the day.

The pellets of **Eagle Owls** can be more than 10 cm long and up to 4 cm wide. They are greyish and can contain very large bone remnants, making them less solid and compact than those of other owls.

It is sometimes difficult to distinguish owl pellets from the scat of other predators, and this is especially true about **fox scat**. Normally the fresh scat of mammalian predators is dark but bleaches over time. In mammal scat, the hair of prey is compressed and lies along the length of the scat, and the scat itself often has an elongated point.

*A **Hawk Owl** regurgitating. HS.*

A **Common Buzzard** *eating a Red Squirrel. HS.*

Raptor pellets

Raptors digest bones more efficiently than owls, and this is why their pellets contain only hair, feathers, and a few bone fragments. Unlike owls' pellets, those of raptors will often contain parts of a bird's beak or claw. They are usually found in large quantities near raptor nests and roosts.

Common Buzzards' pellets are 6–7 cm long and 2–3 cm wide, normally rounded at one end but sometimes pointed at both. They consist of small, grey, whorled pieces of compacted animal hair, and you find them in open fields, below trees, or near fence posts and telephone poles.

Goshawk pellets are about the same size as Common Buzzard's, approximately 5–7 cm long, and they also contain animal hair and bird feathers and are found near nests or below lookout perches.

Kestrels' pellets are significantly smaller, about 3–3.5 cm long and 1.5 cm wide, rounded at one end and pointed at the other. They may, however, also be spherical. In addition to mouse hair and feathers they also contain the remains of insects, especially those of large beetles; you find them in attic areas in disused buildings, church steeples, under kestrel boxes or near the poles and trees on which the birds roost.

The pellets of **Sparrowhawks** and **Hobbys** are 2–4 cm long and 1.2–1.7 cm wide and contain twisted mouse hair and bird feathers. They are almost always found in woodland, especially at woodland edges, and often in large quantities at a single location.

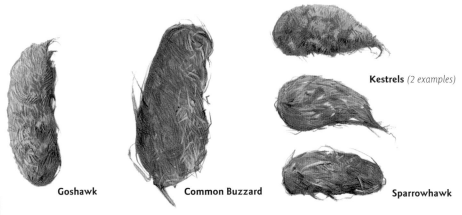

Kestrels (*2 examples*)

Goshawk   **Common Buzzard**   **Sparrowhawk**

*Pellet of a **Herring Gull** containing fish bones. ET.*

Gull, cormorant, heron, and stork pellets

Gulls are omnivorous, and their pellets are loose, since they normally contain no feathers or hairs to bind them. The pellets are normally spherical or short and cylindrical. At the shore, gull pellets will almost always contain fish remnants as well as shell fragments of snails, mussels, or crabs, and they may often be dry and crumbly. Gull pellets further inland contain the remains of a variety of plants and insects and are usually more solid. You find them mainly near breeding colonies and roost sites. The pellets of **Black-headed Gulls** and **Common Gulls** can also be found in fields where birds have been foraging for food.

Pellets of **Herring Gulls** are 3–5 cm long and 2.5–3 cm wide and contain the remains of fish, crabs, mussels, snails, and plants.

Black-headed Gull
(4 examples)

Cormorant

Stork

Herring Gull

Grey Heron

Common Gull
(2 examples)

Pellets of a **Common Gull** *containing cherry stones. PB.*

The pellets of **Common Gulls** are 5–8 cm long and about 2 cm wide, and their contents are similar to those of Black-headed Gulls. When a Common Gull has eaten cherries, the pellets may contain almost nothing but cherry stones.

The pellets of **Black-headed Gulls** are 2.5–4 cm long and 1.5–2 cm wide, and may contain fish bones, the remains of various shore animals, and plants and insects, particularly beetles. When a Black-headed Gull has eaten blueberries and crowberries, the pellets may be a deep blue-black, and

if it has feasted on earthworms, the pellets may contain a lot of earth.

The pellets of **Storks** are more regular in shape than those of herons. They are 4.5–5 cm long and 2.5–3.5 cm wide. Like raptors, storks can digest the bones of their prey, so you will find only hair, feathers, and insect remains in their pellets. The pellets often contain considerable amounts of earth, since storks feed heavily on earthworms. When fresh, the pellets have a sickly sweet, unpleasant odor. They are found mainly near nests.

Herons nest and roost colonially in trees, and you usually find the pellets under trees in a heronry.

The pellets vary considerably; they are often tight and compact, but they may also be elongated, 10 cm or more in length. Bones of birds, mammals, and fish can be digested by Grey Herons; teeth and claws, however, are not digestible. The pellets usually contain the hair of Common and Northern Water Voles and shrews, as well as the remains of insects and some bird feathers.

Common Gull. *BG.*

You find **Cormorant** pellets around colonies and nesting areas, and beneath the trees in which they roost. The trees can become completely white as a result of the birds' droppings and may even die (see p. 45).

Cormorants live almost exclusively on fish, and their pellets usually contain only fish bones and scales. Occasionally you will find the porcelain-like bones of a fish's auditory tract, as well as the shells of mussels and snails, packed in a very slimy and tough case that becomes grey and hard once it dries.

Cormorant. *SDL.*

Raven. *AK.*

Some crows and jays breed in large colonies, and these are good places to find many pellets, particularly under nests.

Wader, crow, and jay pellets

All crows and jays produce pellets, and they are reasonably similar, although, depending on season, their contents will differ greatly. In summer, they often contain vegetable remains, for example grain and cherry stones, as well as remnants of insects and snails, in addition to feathers and carrion. Now and then they may contain stones or pebbles, which are used in the gizzard to grind food into smaller, more digestible fragments. The pellets are normally yellowish and fall apart easily.

Raven *pellets. LG.*

Rook

Jackdaw

Oystercatcher

Magpie

Carrion Crow

The pellets of **Carrion Crow** are 3–7 cm long and 1–2 cm wide and typically found near nests, in fields, and along the beach.

Rook pellets are 3–4 cm long and 1–1.5 cm wide and usually found near rookeries, which can be large and very loud.

Jackdaw pellets are 2.5–3 cm long and 1–1.5 cm wide and normally found near their nests.

Jackdaws will often construct their own nests, which they fill with a selection of large twigs, mainly in hollow trees or on chimneys. Jackdaws are not particularly timid around humans and will sometimes hunt small animals in thatched roofs, consequently dislodging the thatch, which then falls to the ground.

The pellets of **Magpies** are 3.5–4.5 cm long and 1–2 cm wide and generally found under the trees where they nest. Magpies build nests out of twigs and branches high up in trees in urban areas. The nest consists of a basic shell stuffed with plants, hair, paper, etc., and above this a roof of loosely intertwined branches. Normally the female builds the nest while the male provides the materials. Unlike a squirrel's nest, which is built close to the trunk, Magpies build their nests further out, on or between branches (see p. 93).

Oystercatcher pellets are about the same size as those of Magpies, but they fall apart easily since they usually contain fine sand.

Oystercatchers. *BG.*

Tawny Owl *pellets containing 3 mouse skulls. LG.*

Skulls in pellets

Occasionally you come across one or more skulls in a pellet. It is not that easy to identify skulls of particular species, but examination with a magnifying glass can help. If a skull has canines and numerous incisor-like teeth with red tips, and no gap between the front teeth and those behind them, it belongs to an insect eater, so it's likely to be a mole or a shrew. If the skull has no canines, and the front teeth are chisel-shaped and yellowish, and there are gaps between the front teeth and those behind, then it belongs to a rodent.

The skull of a **Common Mole** *is about 30 mm long, the lower jaw about 20 mm. Moles have relatively long and powerful canines and narrow cheekbones.*

A **shrew**'s *skull is up to 20 mm long, the lower jaw up to 12 mm. Shrews have no long canines, and they have no cheekbones.*

The skull of a **Red Squirrel** *is about 40 mm long, the lower jaw about 25 mm. A squirrel has four large molars in each jaw, and the skull is domed.*

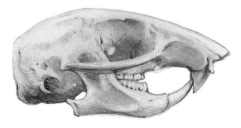

Snowy Owl *pellets. SS.*

An **Eagle Owl**. *HS.*

Long-eared Owl *pellet. EH.*

A **rat**'s skull is 30–40 mm long, the lower jaw about 25 mm long. Rats have three knobbly molars on each side of the jaw, and the skull is flat.

The skull and teeth of a **Bank Vole** are similar to those of a **Northern Water Vole** but smaller, only 20 mm long at most. **Common Vole, Bank Vole, Grey-sided Vole, Northern Water Vole,** and **Norway Lemming** all belong to the same family.

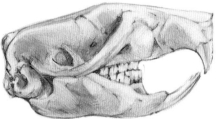

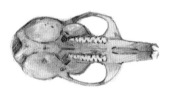

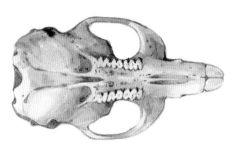

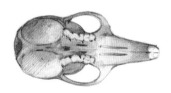

The skull of a **Northern Water Vole** is about 40 mm long and has three curved teeth on each side of the jaw that are shaped like a zigzag if seen from above. The skull is flat.

The skulls and knobbly teeth of the Old World mice resemble those of rats, but are smaller, only 20 mm long at most. The **House Mouse, Wood Mouse, Yellow-necked Mouse, Striped Field Mouse,** and **Harvest Mouse,** among others, are all members of the group known as Old World mice.

Other skulls and bones

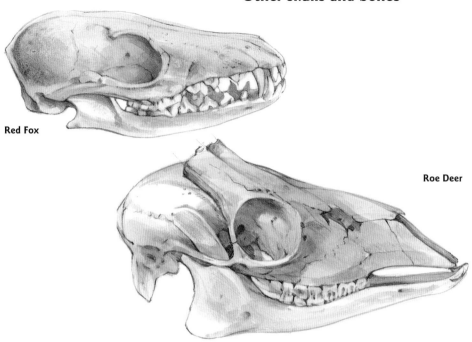

Red Fox

Roe Deer

Larger **mammal** skulls are easier to identify because of their size and other distinctive characteristics. Both the skull and the bones are heavy. Skulls with powerful canines and sharp, pointed molars are most often those of predators, while the skulls of many plant eaters lack both canines and front teeth in the upper jaw.

The skulls and bones of **birds** are very light and can almost float in water; birds also have a relatively large, strong breast bone (clavicle). The size of the skull and the general shape and structure of the beak can help identify the species or family of bird.

*Breast bone of a **swan**. AK.*

*The skull of a **Mountain Hare**. AK*

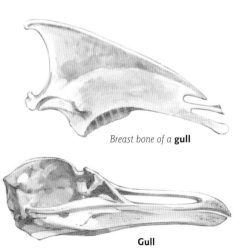

*Breast bone of a **gull***

Gull

Round nests

In the summer, a **Harvest Mouse** weaves a nest out of grass stems. Both photos, LG.

The nest of a **Common Dormouse**, here in a blackberry bush, made out of hay, bark, moss, and lichens. LG.

Squirrels build several types of nests—a main nest as well as several simpler nests used as sleeping quarters. PB.

The **Penduline Tit** *builds a spherical nest in thick underbrush.*

A **Fieldfare** *in its nest. HS.*

A **Magpie**'s *nest. LG.*

The **Garden Dormouse** builds a spherical nest out of branches, leaves, and moss, often inside an old nest box.

Garden Dormouse. L-HL.

The **Pygmy Shrew** builds a summer nest in a hollow tree stump filled with dry grass. Biopix.

A **Marsh Tit** at its nest in a hollow tree. CM.

Nests of **wrens.** Both photos, HS.

Young **spiders** *on a web. AK.*

Witches' broom *is found on birches and from a distance may resemble bird or squirrel nests. The small, closely bunched twigs are stimulated to grow by an infection caused by fungi, viruses, or mites. In Scandinavia you can see them on Asian black birches and, further south, also on weeping birches. AK.*

A web with **caterpillars**. *AK.*

Nest of a **Common Dormouse**.

*Feather of a **Mute Swan**. LG.*

Feathers

Instead of having fur, birds have feathers. They contribute to a bird's appearance and protect its body from cold, sun, rain, and wind. The feathers grow from a kind of pouch (an umbrella-like sheath) and come in two forms, contour and down feathers. Contour feathers are body feathers and the stiffer wing and tail feathers. The wing feathers allow the bird to move, while the tail feathers allow it to brake and steer. The contour feathers often have characteristic colours and patterns, and underneath they can be like down. Down is often dappled, whitish, grey, or brownish.

The feather consists of a shaft and two vanes. The feather is hollow at the root. Each vane has very closely placed barbs, which in turn have two rows of smaller barbules. In the case of contour feathers, the barbules have tiny microscopic hooks, the barbicels, on the side of the tip, and they interlock, forming a coherent surface, the vane. In the down feathers, the barbules have no barbicels.

Some birds have special, somewhat unusual feathers. **Nightjars** have evolved bristle feathers in the area around the beak that make it easier to detect and catch insects. **Herons, bitterns,** and **raptors** have special 'powder' down that grows continuously; it is not lost during moult but instead crumbles into a fine powder at the tip of the feather, which the birds then use when preening. **Woodpeckers** possess tail feathers with a strengthened shaft that can carry a large part of the bird's weight and support it on tree trunks. The tail feathers lack the tip on the shaft.

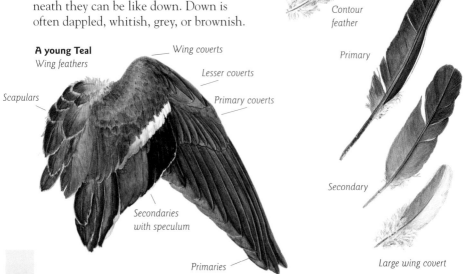

Wood Pigeon

Contour feather

Primary

Secondary

Large wing covert

A young Teal
Wing feathers

Scapulars

Wing coverts

Lesser coverts

Primary coverts

Secondaries with speculum

Primaries

Since feathers wear out and bleach, they occasionally have to be replaced, normally once a year. During moult, old feathers are lost and replaced by new ones. In most species this occurs between the end of summer and the beginning of autumn as they change from summer to winter plumage. Numerous aquatic birds—**ducks, geese, swans, grebes,** and **loons**—lose all their feathers at once and cannot fly for several weeks, so they stay on the water to avoid predators; as a consequence you can often find large quantities of washed-up feathers on shorelines or river banks.

Some male birds with colourful breeding plumage moult their body feathers in the spring but keep their old wing and tail feathers. In Scandinavia, **Willow Ptarmigan** moult their feathers three times a year. Male **Mallards** also go through three yearly moults, while male **Long-tailed Ducks** moult their feathers four times a year.

Great Spotted Woodpecker. *LG.*

Contour feather with down   *Curled upper tail covert feather*   *Secondary with speculum feather*

Male **Mallard**. *LG.*

Scapular feather

Primary feather

Undertail covert feather

Tail feather with reinforced shaft for support on trees

Many male **passerines** lose (abrade) the tips of their body feathers in spring. At this time of year, male **Chaffinches** have a mixture of red, green, and blue feathers, but in winter, males and females look almost identical. **Starlings** lose their yellow spots in the spring and become blue-black in breeding plumage.

Some bird species lose their down during the breeding season, and you can easily see this, especially among terrestrial breeders, for example in colonies of **gulls** and **terns**. The down is used to cushion the nest, so the warmth from the parent's body is transmitted directly to the eggs and young chicks. In **Eider** nests you can find copious amounts of down, the traditional source of stuffing for pillows and duvets.

Raptors and owls moult individual feathers over the course of the year, so they are able to hunt without interruption. Female **Sparrowhawks** and **Peregrine Falcons** moult their plumage during the breeding season, while the males, who bring the food, will moult later. This is why the female's feathers can be found in large quantities near the nest.

Bullfinch. *JL.*

Contour feather (breast)

Wing covert feather

Common Buzzard

Primary feather

Down (contour feather)

Tawny Owl. *AK.*

Primary feather

Secondary feather

Secondary feather

Magpie

Primary feather

Secondary feather with wax-like tip to shaft

Tail feather

Large wing covert feather

Inner secondary feather

Waxwing. *LG.*

Blackbird
Primary feather

Chaffinch
Primary feather

Great Tit
Tail feather

Jay. *Lesser covert feather. LG.*

Raptor feeding signs

Many mammalian predators bite off and then eat the head of a bird after killing it. The feathers are then torn off in clumps, with some feathers stuck together by the predator's saliva. You can recognise the bite marks on larger feathers, and often the whole area where the feather attaches to the bird's body is torn or damaged. The outer sections of the wings may be bitten off; if this is the case, primary feathers will almost separate from the rest of the wing and be connected only by small strips of skin, and the same goes for the tail. The larger bones often show obvious signs of attack.

A raptor often begins by tearing open the head of its avian prey and eating the brain, leaving the beak and remains of the

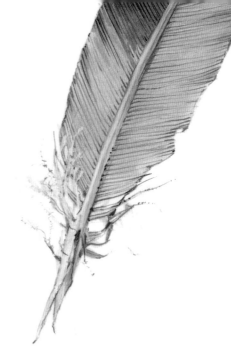

A feather ripped off a bird by a raptor. Note the obvious beak marks on the lower part of the feather.

A **duck** *devoured by a raptor. ST.*

Short-eared Owl *feeds almost exclusively on Common Voles. HS.*

skull. The raptor then plucks the feathers of its victim, tearing out large feathers individually while leaving the rest undamaged. You can often see the place where a raptor tore at feathers because they will be broken or bent. Raptors leave lots of feathers and down behind after plucking and eating their prey.

Normally the breast muscles are eaten first; the raptor cuts wedge-shaped chunks out of the breast, leaving clear marks on the carcass. Raptors do not eat the larger bones and normally also leave the bowels and stomach.

During the breeding season, most raptors pluck their prey at a distance from the nest so as not to reveal its location. After plucking, they carry pieces to their mate

*A dead **hare** with telltale signs of raptor predation. EHA.*

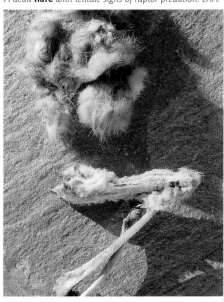

*A **Kestrel** with a Siskin. HS.*

*A **Sparrowhawk** has caught a Tree Sparrow. HS.*

or young. In this case, the skeleton will be missing from the plucking site; thus, discarded pieces of skeleton may be found below the nest.

Some raptors pluck their victims high in the trees, and the feathers are spread far and wide by the wind.

The sites where **Sparrowhawks** and **Goshawks** pluck their prey are similar,

usually in open areas. The prey is taken to a clearing or a woodland edge, placed in a hole in a tree or on a stump or stone or clump of grass, and then plucked. The plucking sites of Goshawks are widely scattered throughout their territory during the breeding period; for the rest of the year they may be much closer together.

Ospreys prefer eating their prey on a favourite tree or post, a position from which they enjoy a good all-round view. Below these sites you will find plentiful droppings and the remains of dead fish.

Plucking sites of **Peregrine Falcons** are always easily accessible in open areas or up in the trees. They normally eat only the breast meat and leave the rest, and they don't pluck the wing feathers; overall, the victim's skeleton is not too badly mangled.

The remains of a raptor kill are quickly discovered by Ravens, crows, gulls, foxes and other carrion eaters, which is why you rarely find more than feathers at the plucking sites.

*An **Osprey** with a common rudd. MH.*

*The remains of a **Peregrine Falcon**'s meal.*

Frog ovaries and spawn. EHA.

Shrikes 'larder' food, skewering their prey on thorns on bushes and trees, even on barbed wire. A larder may contain dead beetles and other large insects, or lizards, mice, and other small rodents.

In the spring, in meadows and moors and along rivers and streams, you can find white or light red clumps of slime on the ground. These are frog ovaries that have been left behind by Common Buzzards, Western Polecats, or mink. These clumps dry in the sun, but swell again in damp weather.

*A **Goshawk** with a Coot. HHN.*

*A **Great Grey Shrike** with its skewered prey. The bird can dismember its prey and still use both legs for balance. HJE. Inset: A shrike has skewered a grasshopper. SDL*

Smashed snail shells in the workshop of a **Song Thrush**. *LG.*

On the ground near a stone or large fallen branch, or on a tree stump, you may occasionally come across piles of broken snail shells. This is the feeding site of a **Song Thrush**, a snail slaughterhouse. The thrush can't peck the shell open, so it strikes it against a hard surface to break it open and get at the contents.

One can find similar workshops at the shore, where gulls or crows have opened mussels, snails, crabs or sea urchins: they carry them high in the air and then drop them on stones or a concrete structure.

Trails

In the wild, most animals follow specific paths where they can move with the least effort, their favoured trails. The animals know these trails intimately, and they will use them to evade predators. When trails are used frequently, they become conspicuous; and different species may share the same trails.

Song Thrushes *strike the shell against a hard surface and eat the contents. AC.*

A **Wild Boar** *trail. AK.*

Mammals

Brown Bear
Ursus arctos

Apart from Polar Bear, which can be found only in Spitsbergen, in the Svalbard Islands of Norway, Brown Bear is the largest terrestrial carnivore in Europe. Standing upright, it can reach a height at the shoulder of 90–125 cm. The female can be up to 2 m long, the male up to 2.35 m; females weigh between 60 and 200 kg, males between 100 and 200 kg. The short tail measures 5–15 cm.

In Scandinavia, Brown Bear lives in conifer forest at higher elevations, preferring old fir forest with clearings and rocks. In central and southern Europe, you find Brown Bear in fir and mixed forest at higher elevations in inaccessible mountain areas.

Outside the mating season and the period during which a female raises her young, bears are mostly solitary and occupy large territories they defend against other bears. They spend winter well hidden during hibernation, often beneath snow.

A bear's tracks are large and hard to confuse with those of any other animal. The prints of the front feet are short and wide, up to 21 cm wide and 18 cm long. The heel prints are not always visible. The prints of the rear feet are longer and slightly narrower, up to 27 cm long and 17 cm wide. The bear has five toes on each foot. The toes are arranged in a slight arc in front of the pads, and the marks of the long, powerful claws are clearly recognisable. The bear's stride is about 90–140 cm long.

A wild bear is a rare sight. AK.

If one disregards the claw marks, the prints of a bear's hind feet resemble those of a human. The bear's innermost toe, which corresponds to a human's big toe, is, however, the smallest on a bear's foot. The tracks of young bears are similar to those of Wolverines or Eurasian Badgers.

Brown Bears are omnivores, but the majority of their diet comprises plant matter; they feed on succulent wild plants, berries, fruit, seeds, and nuts. They also consume a wide variety of ant species (*Formica*), large beetles, and other insects, which they dig out of the forest floor. In Scandinavia, they also hunt large herbivores such as Elk, Reindeer, and other deer species, in southern Europe mainly deer, but also rodents and amphibians, and bears will dig up wasp or bumblebee nests. Brown Bear will feed on the remains of a kill left by

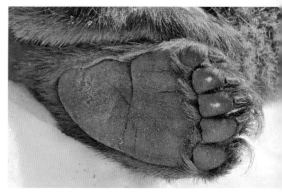

Hind foot of a Brown Bear. Biopix.

other predators and also most other carrion, and they often bury it for later consumption. Occasionally, a Brown Bear might kill a domestic animal such as a sheep or cow.

Bear tracks in sand. TL.

Bear tracks in snow. LG.

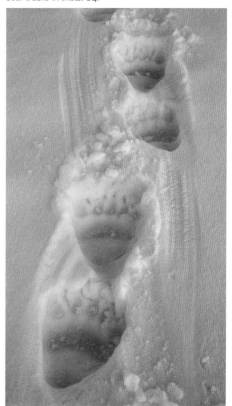

Bear scat. UR.

A bear's scat faithfully reveals its diet. Easily recognisable because of its size, the scat may be mushy or firm. The mushy scat is similar to an Elk's summer scat, but since bears often lick themselves clean, you will almost always find hair in bear scat. The sausage-shaped droppings are 4–5 cm thick.

The scat is left in many places, but it can often be plentiful near a mass of carrion where the bear has been feeding.

A thoroughly ransacked ants' nest is a clear sign of a bear. The top of the nest is almost always removed first, and then the bear digs up everything else in its hunt for ants (see p. 76).

The bear scratches trees with its large claws and also rubs itself against trunks and chews off the bark. A tree with these telltale signs is often called a 'bear tree'. A bear leaves horizontal gnaw marks, whereas scrape markings made by an Elk run vertically. A bear will also bite off small spruce twigs to cushion a bed for itself under the tree. You almost always find longer body hairs at these locations. The bear's winter den is usually well hidden. The den may be located beneath an ants' nest, under the root bole of a downed tree, or in a rock crevice or cave or similar cavity. The ground in the den is cushioned with moss, branches, and dried grass.

Winter snow covers the entrance to the den and helps protect the bear from the cold. A winter den will always be full of the animal's hairs.

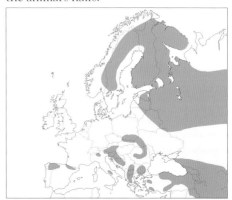

*A **Brown Bear**'s den may be extremely large.*

Wolverine tracks in the mountains. LAD.

Wolverine

Gulo gulo

The Wolverine, the largest European marten, is a powerfully built animal with short legs and a wide, flat head. It stands about 40–45 cm at the shoulder and is about 70–85 cm long. The tail is about 15–25 cm long. The female weighs about 10 kg; the male averages about 15 kg but may weigh up to, and sometimes more than, 25 kg. The Wolverine is not considerably larger than a Eurasian Badger.

With its thick dark fur, the Wolverine appears larger than it actually is. In the area around the eyes there is often a light, yellowish patch, and it has a yellowish stripe running from the shoulders to the tail. Unlike the hairs of dogs or wolves, those of a Wolverine don't bunch together in a clump, even when the animal is wet. This is the reason the fur was once used for the cuffs of sleeves and edging of hoods on windbreakers.

The Wolverine lives in high mountain ranges and in high-elevation rugged wooded areas. It is territorial, marking the boundaries of its territory with scent secretions. Other than the mating season

or when the female is raising young, the Wolverine is solitary. It does not hibernate, but rests in caves on rocky slopes, under large rocks, or in abandoned fox dens, or even digs a lair in a pile of snow at the bottom of a slope.

The Wolverine covers a wide area searching for food. Like other marten species, it moves with a jumping gait, and you normally find prints of all four feet. The normal stride is 60–120 cm, but when it walks or trots in snow, the Wolverine places the hind feet in or very close to the tracks of the front feet, reducing the length of its stride.

A Wolverine rolls on the ground to scratch its back. LS.

109

Wolverines have an excellent sense of smell. ME.

A Wolverine can climb like a bear. ME.

The Wolverine is an omnivore but will kill a wide range of prey including Reindeer, deer, sheep, small rodents, hares, frogs, birds, and larger insects. It readily consumes carrion, often carcasses left by Lynx or wolves. Wolverines will often cache the remains of larger animals. In late summer, Wolverines consume many berries.

The Wolverine caches food for winter. Just like Brown Bear, the Wolverine can chew the bark and branches off small trees, possibly also as a way to mark its territory.

The tracks are large, since the sole of the foot is covered with long, insulating hairs. Both the front and rear feet have five toes with long, powerful claws, but the imprint of the inner toe may sometimes be missing. The track can resemble that of a dog or small bear, though the toes usually form an arc in the front footprint. The front footprint is larger, at 12–16 cm long and 7–8 cm wide. Because the Wolverine lacks a heel pad, the rear footprints are narrower and shorter.

The twisted scat, up to 15 cm long and about 2.5 cm thick, often contain hairs and shards of bone. As is the case with the scat of other marten species, it is pointed at one end and left to mark territory. Unlike other marten species, the Wolverine does not use latrines.

A sheep killed by a Wolverine. BW.

Wolf and domestic dog
Canis lupus

The Wolf's body is 100–145 cm long, the tail about 50 cm. The female weighs about 30–35 kg, the male normally 35–45 kg, but may reach 75 kg. The height at the shoulder is approximately 70–80 cm. The fur is yellow-grey, darker on the back, with black areas on shoulders, haunches, and tail. The legs are light, the belly yellowish or grey-white. The winter coat is lighter. On the upper side of the tail, just below the base, there is a black spot.

In its appearance the Wolf resembles a German Shepherd or a large German Spitz, even a Greenland Husky; however, the Wolf has longer legs, and the front feet are closer together. A Wolf's tracks are therefore not as wide as a domestic dog's. Normally, the dominant wolves in a pack keep their tails raised, while the others keep theirs lowered.

Wolves are pack animals and often hunt in the dark. Above, LG; below, ME.

Wolves live in family packs with a dominant male and female and their offspring, but they may also gather in larger packs that patrol clearly demarcated territories, especially in winter. Wolves prefer open terrain with isolated groups of trees rather than dense woodland.

The tracks of a Wolf can resemble those of a large dog or a Lynx; however, Wolf tracks are elongated, while a dog's are more rounded. Lynx tracks show no claw marks, and the footprints are asymmetric. Wolf tracks may also resemble those of a fox but are much larger. The Wolf has five toes on the front foot, but the innermost toe is located too high to be visible in the prints. The hind foot has only four toes. The front footprints of both Wolves and large domestic dogs are larger, about 9–11 cm long and 8–10 cm wide; the tracks of the hind feet are about 8 cm long and 7 cm wide. The stride is about 90–20 cm; when running, about 120–160 cm.

The toe pads of a Wolf are longer than those of a dog, and the two middle toes are more markedly splayed; the claw marks are also stronger, longer, and more pointed. If one were to draw a straight line between the prints of the two foremost (middle) toes, this line would always cross the prints of the two outer toes (*cf.* p. 7). With Red Fox, the line will lie behind the prints of the most forward toes and immediately in front of the two hind ones.

Both Wolf and Red Fox frequently place their hind feet in the prints made by the front, so the tracks form a line that is almost straight. A dog often runs with its body slightly canted, so the prints of the hind feet will lie slightly outside those of the front.

Wolf tracks in deep snow. Below left, ME; right, UR.

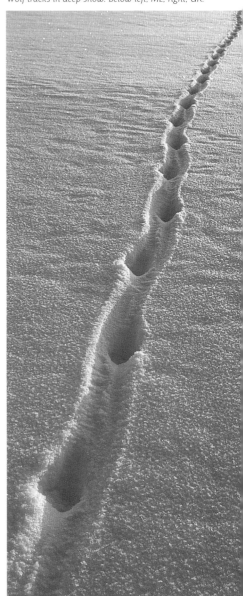

Wolf prints in the sand. DS.

Hind foot of a Wolf. LG.

The tracks of a Wolf often follow a long straight path, while a dog's prints will inevitably veer left or right when the animal is distracted by an interesting smell or by marking its territory. The Wolf is a heavy animal and sinks deep into fresh snow, which is why several Wolves will follow one another and use the same path—and of course domestic dogs seldom run in a pack.

The scat of a Wolf is the same size as a dog's and cylindrical in shape, often dark grey, 10–15 cm long, 2.5–3 cm thick, slightly twisted, and often pointed at the ends. When a Wolf has eaten freshly killed prey, the scat can be almost black and soft. It often contains identifiable remains of the prey, while a dog's scat is not twisted and contains no recognisable remains of its food.

The Wolf defecates at resting places or at the boundaries of its territory, and the scat is clearly visible on stones, stumps, and the like where it has marked its territory; the tracks of the hind feet dragging across the ground may also be visible at these locations. Fresh scat has a markedly musty odor.

The Wolf uses urine to mark the borders of its territory on stones, trees, or other

A Wolf's den. LG.

A female Wolf marking territory. LG.

prominent spots. Exactly in the fashion of a domestic dog, the male lifts its leg, while the female urinates in a squatting position.

A Wolf's den has certain characteristics: the entrance is large enough to allow quick entry and exit, and it is usually deep in sandy terrain or between rocks, under tree roots, or in other natural cavities.

A pack has access to several dens within the home territory, but only one is used when the wolves have cubs. If the pack feels threatened, it moves to another den. Once the cubs are weaned, they join the pack and move around the territory. Wolves often rest in specific locations and flatten the grass by regular use. Wolves readily eat large animals such as Elk or Reindeer, but they also hunt hares, rabbits, European Beavers, and small rodents. You will come across kills throughout a territory and also abundant tracks and scat.

A deer killed by a Wolf. LGA.

A Lynx stalking prey. ME.

Lynx

Lynx lynx

Lynx tracks. SJ.

The Lynx is a wary, shy animal and rarely seen. It is 60–75 cm tall at the shoulder and 80–130 cm long, with a tail measuring about 11–25 cm. It weighs 16–38 kg, the male being considerably larger than the female. The head is small, light brown or orange-brown, but with paler, whitish cheeks. The Lynx has white eye rings, while the 'eyebrows' are long and black. It has large ears with dark tufts, and there is a white spot on the back of each ear. In summer its back, sides, and legs are light brown or orange-brown with dark spots, the belly grey-white; in winter, the coat is generally lighter. The tail is spotted and ends in a dark tip.

Normally the Lynx is solitary within a large territory. In the north of its range it prefers mature open woodland with some rock cover; in southern Europe it favours woodland with a thick underbrush. During the day it rests at a look-out spot and then begins hunting at dusk.

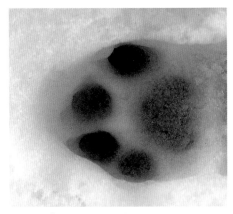

Footprint of a Lynx in snow. JLI.

The Lynx has four toes on each foot and normally retracts its claws when it walks. The forefoot is slightly larger than the hind. The tracks are 7–9 cm long and about the same width. The print of the innermost of the two middle toes is set slightly apart from those of the other toes. As a Lynx moves forward, it usually places its hind feet in the tracks of the front, leaving a track that forms almost a straight line. When hunting, a Lynx might jump energetically, and the prints of the

claws will also be visible then. The stride is about 80–100 cm.

Lynx tracks are similar to those of a large domestic cat and may often be distinguished from a domestic dog or cat only with difficulty. Hairs on the bottom of the Lynx's foot make the print more circular, and the marks of the foot pad do not quite reach the edge of the footprint.

Lynx hunt hares, rabbits, foxes, Reindeer, and other deer species, but it also takes small rodents, squirrels, and birds. Smaller animals are consumed almost completely, while the carcasses of larger prey are left where they were killed. The Lynx eats as much as it can and then leaves the remains for other carrion eaters. The carcass may be cached under earth, moss, or snow; the Lynx will return to it later.

You only rarely find Lynx scat, since it is usually buried, but it may be found at the edges of an individual's territory. It is up to 25 cm long and 3 cm thick and may contain hair, feathers, and the remains of bones. When scat is fresh it is pungent.

A Lynx has killed a Reindeer with a bite to the throat. TL.

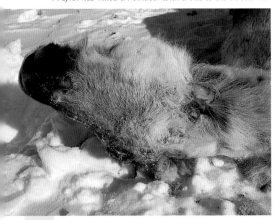

Iberian Lynx. WWE.

Iberian Lynx

Lynx pardinus

The Iberian Lynx is smaller than the Lynx, slimmer and with longer legs. It is about 85–100 cm long and stands 60–70 cm tall at the shoulder; the tail measures about 60–70 cm,. The female weighs up to 10 kg, the male about 13 kg, but the latter may weigh up to 26 kg. The coat is light grey-brown with pronounced dark spots. The whiskers and ear tufts are longer than those of Lynx. The footprints are similar to those of Lynx, and the same is true of the scat.

The Iberian Lynx lives in open woodland with underbrush; it hunts mainly wild rabbits, but also hares, rodents, birds, reptiles, and amphibians. This is one of the most endangered cats in the world; its habitat is threatened, and only very small populations remain in southern Spain.

Wildcat

Felis silvestris

The Wildcat is an extremely shy predator and seen only very rarely, and it cannot be domesticated. The coat is long, soft and thick, grey or yellowish grey with dark stripes. The Wildcat is about 48–80 cm long and the tail about 26–37 cm; the cat weighs about 5–10 kg. The male weighs a little more than the female, up to 15 kg. The tail is bushy and rather blunt, with dark rings and a black tip. The Wildcat resembles a very large domestic cat, but has longer legs; the height at the shoulder is about 35–40 cm.

The Wildcat lives in wooded upland areas, where it finds shelter in dens between rocks and stones, under roots, in hollow trees, or in thick underbrush. It is mostly nocturnal, but during the day it can sometimes be seen basking in the sun.

The Wildcat has five toes on the front feet and four on the hind. The toes have sharp claws that are normally retracted

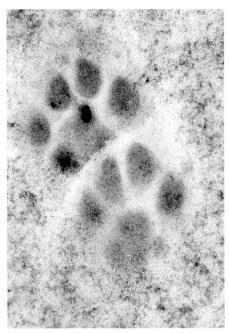

As it moves, the Wildcat places its hind feet immediately behind the front feet. EHA.

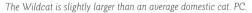

The Wildcat is slightly larger than an average domestic cat. PC.

when the cat is moving. The prints of front and hind feet are almost the same, because the inner toe on the front foot is located too high to leave a print. The footprints are circular, about 4–6 cm long and 3.5–5 cm wide. The Wildcat moves quietly in its territory, but can jump energetically when hunting. The tracks basically follow a straight line, and the stride is about 30–60 cm.

The Wildcat preys mainly on hares, rabbits, rodents, and small birds, as well as some insects. It swallows small animals whole, but with larger animals, the cat eats only the flesh and leaves the bones behind. Smaller animals may be cached under moss or earth, but the Wildcat rarely returns to carrion. The scat is normally buried or covered with earth and plants; at the edge of the territory it may be left in the open on stones or tree trunks. The scat is 4–8 cm long and 1.5 cm thick, often segmented and with pointed ends. It contains hair, bone, and insect remains, and when fresh smells very pungent. The Wildcat sharpens its claws by scratching trees, the same way Lynx and domestic cats do. The bark abrades the outermost layer of the nails, sharpening them in the process. Scratch marks

The Wildcat sharpens its claws on tree trunks. PB.

on tree trunks are a sign to other Wildcats that this territory is occupied. Wildcats also mark their territory with scent. Many Wildcat 'scratching trees' might be found well inside an individual's territory, away from other cats, so this is more a sign that the cat is simply flexing its muscles and stretching rather than marking its territory.

Wildcat scat, used here to mark territory. AD.

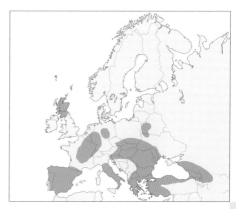

Tracks of an Arctic Fox in the Norwegian mountains—a rare sight. RM.

Arctic Fox
Alopex lagopus

The Arctic Fox is somewhat smaller than Red Fox, with shorter snout, tail, and ears, and sturdier legs. The height at the shoulder is about 30 cm and length is about 55–65 cm; the tail is about 30–55 cm

An Arctic Fox in its summer coat. HS.

long, Arctic Fox normally weighs about 3–5 kg but may weigh up to 8 kg.

The Arctic Fox is also known as the Snow Fox, and has two colour morphs; in the summer, the blue morph is grey-brown; in the winter, it is darker, grey-black to dark brown, and almost blue. The white morph is grey-black on the back in the summer, and grey-white on the sides and underbelly. The winter coat is pure white. The Arctic Fox lives in high mountain regions above the treeline. In years with plentiful cubs, individuals may also move into lowland areas. On Svalbard and Iceland, it may also be seen in the coastal regions, where it feeds on flotsam, fish, and crabs, as well as seal and whale carcasses. Like Red Fox, the Arctic Fox is territorial and lives in family groups. In the mountains it feeds mostly on small

Arctic Fox cubs in their summer coats, two white and a blue morph. TSC.

rodents, lemmings for instance, as well as birds and their eggs and young, but also on Reindeer carrion. In the summer it also eats berries. The Arctic Fox is active both day and night but most easily seen at dusk.

The tracks are smaller and more rounded than those of Red Fox, 5–6 cm long and similar to the tracks of a small dog. In winter you see only faint pad prints, since the feet are covered with hair. The claws of the inner toes point inward; the stride is also shorter than that of Red Fox. Arctic Fox moves less at a trot, making more short jumps in the gait, and the prints of all four feet are quite visible. The length of the stride is about 70–100 cm.

The Arctic Fox digs a large den in the open mountain landscape, often with various levels and exits. Prey are carried into the den; when the remains are combined with scat, the earth is well fertilised, and as a consequence, vegetation surrounding the den is often lush and easily visible.

The scat of Arctic Fox resembles that of Red Fox, but is smaller, 1–1.5 cm thick and 5–10 cm long and, because it contains the hair of prey, often grey.

Red Fox

Vulpes vulpes

The back and flanks of Red Fox are reddish or greyish brown, the throat and chest normally white or greyish white, or may be black. The tail ends in a light tip. Red Fox is about 70 cm long, and the tail, about 40 cm. The male weighs about 8 kg, but may reach 15 kg. The female is smaller and weighs about 6.5 kg, rarely reaching 9.5 kg. The height at the shoulder is 35–40 cm.

The Red Fox is most comfortable in open landscapes without thick vegetation, including fields, moorland, and meadows, but it also lives in suburbs and some large cities. You will also find Red Foxes in coastal areas. They are normally active at dusk or at night but regularly seen during the day as well.

The Red Fox lives in an established territory, marked by scat and the animal's strong-smelling urine. The female fox urinates like a female domestic dog, usually on trails; the male cocks his hind leg, also like a dog.

Foxes can live as loners, but normally they live in family groups comprising the adults, the young, and sometimes one or more individuals of lower 'rank'.

Red Foxes feed mainly on small rodents, primarily voles, but small birds,

A Red Fox listens for mice under the snow. ME.

pigeons, game birds, and eggs are also on the menu. The fox can also catch grown hares and deer and their young, when the latter are weak or sick. Carrion such as road kill is also readily consumed, and in summer, earthworms, insects, and fruit and berries are eaten as well. Food put out for pets, hedgehogs, or garden birds may also be taken.

The tracks of Red Fox look like those of small dogs, but the prints are generally longer and narrower. The fox has five toes on the front foot, but the inner toe is set too high to leave a print. The hind foot has four toes. If one draws a straight line behind the two middle pads they will

A fox print in sand. LG.

Fox tracks in snow. LG.

be parallel or in front of the prints of the two rear and outer pads (*cf.* p. 10), but in a domestic dog they are parallel to the rear pads (*cf.* p. 7). The prints of the toe pads are narrower and not as close together as they are for domestic dogs, and the claw prints are sharper than those of a domestic dog.

The footprint of a Red Fox is 5–7 cm long and 4–4.5 cm wide, with the front footprint clearer than that of the hind. The claws on the two middle toes of the front foot are more widely splayed than those on the hind foot. The stride is about 60–90 cm.

When the fox moves quietly through snow, it normally places the hind feet in the tracks of the front feet, while a domestic dog often places them slightly askance. On firm terrain, however, the fox can also move with its feet slightly apart the way a dog does, and you will then see two tracks.

A fox has marked its territory with urine. EHA.

Fox hairs on a barbed wire fence. LG.

Fox scat. ED.

A fox marks its territory by leaving scat in prominent places, one of several strategies for marking. NPHH.

Red Fox tracks normally do not follow a straight line, instead showing numerous side steps; a domestic dog moves in more linear fashion.

If a fox regularly passes by a barbed wire fence, you can often find strands of its hair caught on a barb. The colour, length, and texture clearly reveal the identity of the animal (*cf.* p. 14).

Fox scat is 1.5–2.5 cm wide and 5–10 cm long. It is often segmented, with hair holding the segments together. The scat is lightly twisted and ends in a point. Scat is used to mark territory and often left in prominent places—in the middle of a path, on a stone or a molehill. Fresh scat has a strong odour. The scat contains the remains of the fox's meal: hair, feathers, fruit stones, insects, and pieces of bone. As time passes, the scat becomes grey and may resemble an owl's pellet.

Beware! Red Fox scat should not be touched, because it might contain the eggs of a dwarf tapeworm that may be deadly to humans; however, this tapeworm is not as common in northern Europe as it is in central and southern Europe.

The fox gives birth to its young in a den. On open slopes, often with a southern exposure and sandy or gravelly soil, you can see the excavated soil in a long arc below the den's entrance. The entrance is 25–30 cm wide. There is no rut like the one you might see at the entrance of a Eurasian Badger's den. The fox may also utilise natural cavities, or build a den between roots or large rocks or in rock crevices. Garden sheds or outhouses may also be used, as well as old Eurasian Badger or Rabbit burrows. When the den is in use, clear tracks and the remains of prey are easily visible, the grass is usually trampled, and there is a discernible smell of fox.

Signs of digging. LG.

Red Foxes like to rest in front of their den. LG.

A fox consumes mice and small birds whole. In stubble fields you can see places where a fox has found a mouse's nest and dug it out to find the young.

Large birds and mammals are often carried to a place where the fox can eat them undisturbed. When it has caught a larger bird, the fox will often chew off the flight feathers.

Larger animals that the fox cannot carry are cached and marked with urine. When a fox eats eggs, it breaks the shell into large pieces and licks out the contents. Eggs are often hidden under moss and plants for later consumption.

A fox gnawed on this deer corpse. SSU.

The jumps and leaps of a fox are well suited for hunting small rodents. ME.

The Raccoon Dog truly resembles a Raccoon. ATA.

Raccoon Dog

Nyctereutes procyonoides

The Raccoon Dog is native to East Asia; it was brought to European Russia at the beginning of the nineteenth century and has since spread to other parts of Europe. Because of the white area around its snout, it strongly resembles a Raccoon, but the black band on its face is broken into two parts. The forehead is light, and an even lighter, almost white area stretches over the entire neck. The ears have dark borders, the back is mottled grey with dark stripes. The chest, belly, and legs are black, the tail is unstriped and dark on top, light underneath. The legs are all the same length.

Raccoon Dog is about 60–80 cm long, and the tail measures up to 20 cm. Its height at the shoulder is 20–30 cm, and it weighs up to 10 kg. The Raccoon Dog's thick fur exaggerates its true size.

Raccoon Dogs live in deciduous or mixed forest with thick underbrush, usually near water or swamps, and in open landscapes with wet areas and areas with bush cover. It is not a shy animal, so you might also see it near or in inhabited areas.

Raccoon Dogs do not hibernate, but like Eurasian Badgers they remain in their den for several days if there is a severe frost or heavy snow.

The prints of Raccoon Dog always show four toes set an equal distance from the central pad print, as well as clear claw marks. The front footprint is 4–5.5 cm long and about 4.5 cm wide, the rear footprints are somewhat smaller, 4–4.5 cm long and about 3.5 cm wide; the stride is about 40–60 cm.

The tracks can resemble those of a fox, although the latter are more elongated.

There is essentially no visible difference between the tracks of a domestic dog and those of a Raccoon Dog, and the latter may also be confused with the tracks of a domestic cat, even though the cat's footprints never show claw prints.

A male and female often hunt together, and one often sees the prints of two animals in the same place. The footprints are often found on the muddy shores of lakes or streams or in marshy areas. At the water's edge, one may often also find paths that are regularly used by the animals.

Male and female Raccoon Dogs often hunt together. Biopix.

A Raccoon Dog can dig its own den, but it will also use old Eurasian Badger and fox dens, or live in natural cavities: in hollow trees, under roots, or between stones and rocks. One will almost always find the remains of prey close by.

Raccoon Dogs live in family groups in established territories, which are, however, not defended vigorously.

Like Raccoons and Eurasian Badgers, Raccoon Dogs are omnivores, but they consume mainly small rodents. The scat is somewhat twisted, 5–8 cm long, 1.5–2 cm thick, and often contains much hair. It resembles domestic dog scat, but is left in piles—in latrines near the burrow or along the edge of territory.

Beware! Raccoon Dog scat should not be touched since it can contain eggs of the dwarf tapeworm (transmitted by foxes), which can be dangerous to human beings. In many places in eastern Europe, this is the reason mushrooms and berries are not gathered in the wild.

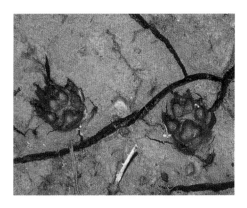

Tracks and scat of Raccoon Dog. AVD.

Raccoon Dogs have five to eight young per litter. Biopix.

Raccoon

Procyon lotor

The Raccoon was introduced from North America to Europe for the fur trade at the beginning of the twentieth century. Escapes over time have multiplied and the naturalised population in Europe has increased steadily.

Raccoons are often confused with the Eurasian Badger, though Raccoons have a black stripe diagonally crossing the area above the eyes, as well as a dark blaze from the snout to the forehead. On the side of the snout there are white areas, and the Raccoon also has white above the eyes. The ears have a light border, and the tail is striped diagonally with six or seven dark stripes which are longer than those on a Eurasian Badger. The coat is grey, brownish, reddish brown, or almost black on the upper side. Raccoons are about 48–70 cm long, and the tail measures about 20–30

A Raccoon in a tree. JH.

cm. Raccoons weigh between 5 and 15 kg. The hind legs are longer than the front, so they move with the hindquarters slightly raised.

Raccoons prefer deciduous woodland or underbrush near lakes, streams, and rivers, but may also be found in other open areas such as parks or arable land. If it is not persecuted, the Raccoon may become quite confiding.

Raccoons are normally solitary but—especially where they are fed by humans—may also live in groups. Raccoons are usually nocturnal; during the day they sleep in hollow trees, rock crevices, and other natural cavities, or even in abandoned Eurasian Badger or fox dens. Raccoons don't hibernate but are noticeably less active in winter than in summer.

Raccoons have long and dexterous fingers, especially those on the front feet. The tracks show the footprints of all five toes and the pads as well as the imprint of powerful claws. Raccoons are good climbers and can rotate their hind feet 180 degrees to maintain their hold, and they are able to climb down trees headfirst. The toes are widely splayed; the front footprint is about 7–7.5 cm long and 6.5–7 cm wide, the hind footprint 8.5–9 cm long and 6–7 cm wide.

A Raccoon's footprints, hind foot and forefoot. BZ.

You can usually find their tracks near places where the Raccoon sleeps during the day: along lakeshores and banks of streams, or along paths where it forages for food. The vegetation can become thoroughly trampled in these areas, especially if young are present. You can also find the animals' hair scattered in these places.

Raccoons feed on mussels and crustaceans in shallow water, but since they are opportunistic omnivores, they also consume fish, frogs, aquatic insects, snails, and aquatic plants, as well as nuts, fruits and berries, vegetables, seeds, small rodents, birds, eggs, and nestlings. Raccoons will also feed on carrion.

Raccoons will break into chicken coops and pheasantries, and they feed on garbage and food left by humans for domestic pets, wild animals, or birds. Lawns can be excavated as they search for insect larvae and worms. Raccoon scat looks like that of a midsized domestic dog. The scat is usually dark, but may change colour depending on diet. The scat is round, 3–8 cm long and 1–2 cm thick, and crumbles easily. It is left in piles near sleeping quarters, in latrines, also along the shores of lakes and banks of streams and rivers, and near fences, hedges, and other man-made obstacles.

Beware! Do not touch a Raccoon's scat since it might contain the eggs of a nematode that can cause dangerous infections in humans.

A Raccoon can become very trusting. JH.

Eurasian Badger

Meles meles

The Eurasian Badger is a common but very shy predator. It is a compact animal with short legs and a long snout, about 30 cm high at the shoulder and 67–90 cm long, and has a tail measuring about 11–20 cm. The weight can vary greatly depending on age, sex, and season. The female weighs between 6 and 14 kg, the male from 9 to 17 kg, but in the autumn, when they are at their heaviest, the male can reach 20 kg.

Eurasian Badgers have a white head with a pronounced black stripe from the snout over the eyes and ears to the back of the neck. The ears have white edges. The coat is mottled grey on the back and sides, the tail mottled a slightly lighter grey, and the belly and legs are black.

Eurasian Badgers prefer mixed woodland with undergrowth and some clearings,

fields, or meadows. They are generally nocturnal, but in the northern regions of Scandinavia the nights are short, so they have to forage during the day.

Eurasian Badgers feed primarily on earthworms, but they also consume insects, snails, frogs, moles, and carrion, and will plunder bird and mouse nests on the ground. They also unearth wasp and bumblebee nests.

A Eurasian Badger setting out to forage. LG.

The print of a Eurasian Badger's front foot, with the hind foot placed on top but slightly further back. VO.

feet are somewhat smaller than those of the front, about 3.5–4 cm long and 4.5 cm wide without the heel pad. When the heel pad is visible, the whole print is about 6.5 cm long. The stride is about 40–60 cm, when trotting, 70–90 cm.

Eurasian Badgers usually move slowly when foraging, placing the hind feet behind the front. When they move quickly, the prints of the hind feet overlap those of the front, and when they run, badgers actually place the hind feet ahead of the front, and all the prints might be clearly distinguished. Unlike other members of the marten family, badgers hardly ever jump.

A Eurasian Badger's scat is black and slimy after it has eaten a lot of

Eurasian Badger tracks. PH.

Eurasian Badgers also eat a variety of plants, especially wild oats, corn, and legumes, as well as fruit and berries.

Eurasian Badgers live in family groups comprising a dominant male with one or more females and their offspring. They live in territories with boundaries marked with scent or scat.

Badgers do not hibernate but may remain in their den for several days when there is a bitter frost or heavy snow.

A badger's prints resemble those of a small bear, but the front footprint is sometimes missing the impression of the ball. Eurasian Badgers have 5 long and powerful toes on each foot. The front footprint is 4–6 cm wide and about 5 cm long, or 7 cm if the heel print is also visible. The claws on the front feet can be up to 3 cm long. The prints of the claws of the 4 outermost toes form an arc separate from the pad, but the prints of the hind claws are generally fainter. The prints of the hind

Straw bedding. LG.

earthworms. If its food sources are more varied, the scat is sausage-shaped, about 2 cm thick and up to 10 cm long. Normally the scat is pointed at one end, but never twisted. It can contain hair, bones, undigested parts of insects, as well as the stones of fruit. The scat is deposited in small latrine trenches about 10–15 cm deep dug along paths either close to the den or along the edge of the territory. The latrine is not covered and is used repeatedly.

The badger builds a burrow system (called a set) that is enlarged each year; it can be several metres deep and have

Eurasian Badger scat. PB.

Latrine of Eurasian Badger. L-HO.

several entrances. The passages can be more than 100 m long in very large sets. The set is often situated on a slope with underbrush, but badgers can also live under abandoned buildings in woodland, or in sheds, garages, etc., at the edges of settlements or in areas with holiday cottages as well as in rocky terrain and in cavities under large rocks.

Inside the set, one or more living quarters are cushioned with dried grass, straw, moss, and the like. The badger drags these materials backwards into the burrow; this is why you always see a deep rut in front of the entrance. Older nesting material is removed and may be found scattered around the entrance.

Unlike fox dens, a badger's set will have no remains of food in the front, and a set does not smell like an active fox den.

There are clear markings on larger trees close to the burrow; this is where the badger cleans earth off its claws. These scratches might also serve as a form of territorial marking.

In the course of foraging, if the badger happens upon a wasp or bumblebee nest, these will be completely excavated. The badger eats larvae and pupae, and occasionally the entire nest. The Honey Buzzard behaves in an identical fashion, so to learn which animal was responsible for the destruction, you must look for other clues; however, Honey Buzzard usually leaves more remains at its nest site than a badger typically would.

When searching for beetle larvae and earthworms, the badger leaves small funnel-shaped holes in the grass with its feet. In cow pastures, the badger flips over or churns up cowpats looking for worms and larvae. Mushrooms may also be knocked over in the search for snails.

Well-trodden paths often lead from the set through the landscape to favoured feeding areas.

A deep rut can always be seen in front of an old badger set. LG.

135

European Beaver
Castor fiber

European Beavers are the largest rodents in Europe. They have streamlined bodies and short legs. They normally weigh between 13 and 21 kg, but females are larger and may weigh up to 35 kg; they are 70–90 cm long, with a tail measuring 25–40 cm long and flat like the blade of an oar; the skin on the tail is scaly and furless.

The beaver's fur is a shiny greyish brown, with strong outer coat over a thicker, softer undercoat. Beavers live near lakes or moving water. They swim around quietly, only the head and a part of the upper back visible. When beavers dive, they may remain under water for 2–3 minutes, but they can also, if threatened, hold their breath for up to 15 minutes.

Beavers feed exclusively on plants. In summer they feed on succulent aquatic plants and their roots, in winter on the bark of a variety of deciduous trees. They prefer ashes, poplars, alders, birches, willows, and mountain ash but may feed on other species. Beavers eat their food in or

A dam ensures the water level stays high above the lodge. LG.

European Beaver uses its flat tail as a rudder in the water. HS.

near the water. In the fall they gather supplies to consume in their lodges.

Beavers live in family groups comprising a male and female and their offspring. They live in territories which they mark with scent. They are most easily seen early in the morning and at dusk, but can be active the entire day if left undisturbed.

The beaver is a mammal that leaves some of the clearest tracks and signs; they are hard to miss on most occasions. Felled trees, cone-shaped stumps, gnawed branches and trunks as well as the beaver's dams and structures are all highly visible.

In Denmark, beavers were exterminated 2,000–2,500 years ago, but they were reintroduced in the Holstebro area in 1999. At that time, 18 animals were released; the population has now grown and spread to the other water bodies in western Jutland, and now also in Seeland. Beavers were almost exterminated across Europe, but thanks to successful reintroduction, they are now no longer threatened in many countries.

Beaver tracks in sand; on the left, a particularly clear impression of a front foot. NPHH.

137

The front foot has five long toes lacking webbing as well as strong, sharp claws; the tracks, however, often show only the prints of four well-splayed toes. The footprints are 5–6 cm long and 4.5 cm wide. The hind feet have webbing between the toes. The second toe has a double claw which the beaver uses to groom its coat. The prints are 15–18 cm long and 10 cm wide.

On land, beavers move slowly and carefully. On soft ground you can often see drag marks left by the tail that can erase the footprints (*cf.* p. 141). The stride is 40–60 cm.

Beavers feel safe in water and avoid going on land whenever possible. For this reason, they dig narrow channels in low-lying, marshy areas where they can carry branches to their feeding sites, lodges, and dams.

Beavers fell trees to gather branches for their constructions and dams, but also to gather leaves and bark to eat. They can fell trees up to 0.5 m in diameter by means of cross-cutting, leaving only a conical stump. The largest gnaw marks are found on the side of a trunk facing water, which is why the trees they gnaw almost always fall in the water.

Beavers set their upper teeth solidly in the tree and then chew out large chips perpendicular to the grain with the lower teeth. Chips 3–4 cm wide and 10–12 cm long lie in large piles next to the tree stumps.

Near the water and in front of felled trees you will often find gnawed branches, so-called beaver-staves. The tooth marks in the trunks and branches are about 8 mm wide.

Beavers can push their lips behind their teeth, preventing water from entering their mouths while they chew. LGA; inset, ME.

Felled trees with large wood chips and a tree trunk with gnaw marks. There are clearly recognisable gnaw marks on the young tree below. LG above; Biopix below.

A beaver family living in running water will build a dam out of branches and trunks, placing it downstream and close to the lodge. The dam is sealed with sod and smaller materials to ensure a high water level in front of and around the lodge. Dams are constructed mostly in the autumn and enlarged and improved every year; they can be up to 100 m long and 2 m high.

Beaver families live in constructions resembling flat pyramids with a diameter of up to 15 m and height up to 2 m. When beavers build structures in embankments, they might be long and flat, but if the structures are in the water, they are always cone-shaped. Sod and earth are packed between branches and trunks to protect the lodge, and older structures can be completely overgrown with plants as a result. The entrance is always located below the water's surface. Inside the lodge, you may find several chambers. In autumn, beavers stockpile branches in front of the lodge, embedding them in muddy ground.

Beavers relish succulent aquatic plants. HS.

Beavers build their lodges in embankments and open areas. AK.

Some beavers do not build lodges in the open but are content with building a den into a steep embankment.

In summer, beavers feed mostly on aquatic plants, their favourite being blue pygmies and their roots. You can see the remains of meals floating in the water. In autumn and winter, beavers feed mostly on the bark of ash and willow, but they also consume the bark of birch and other deciduous trees; they avoid conifers. Tree stumps may be totally peeled of their bark; chewed-off branches—'beaver staves'—can be found in the water.

Beaver scat is brown, almost round, about 2 cm thick and 2–4 cm long. It consists of rough, undigested plant fibres. The scat is left in the water and can frequently be found near feeding sites on the shore or close to the family home.

Beavers leave their scat in the water.

The beaver family marks its territory with castoreum, a strong-smelling scent secretion produced by two glands at the base of the tail. The beaver also has two anal glands. Both castor sacs and anal glands are used to mark territory; secretions are usually left on small piles of material gathered by the animals and left near the water's edge. Scent markings may also be left on felled trees.

The tracks of a beaver tail across a gravel path. PB.

The European Beaver may build its lodge in an embankment. AK.

North American Beaver. HS.

North American Beaver

Castor canadensis

North American Beavers were first released in Finland. They become sexually mature earlier, have more offspring, and therefore live in larger family groups than European Beavers. In Finland they succeeded in displacing European Beavers, and the introduced species is now dominant in that country. From Finland, North American Beavers have spread to Russia, and they might move into Sweden and Norway. There are no differences in the tracks of the two beaver species.

North American Beavers build their lodge over a floating wooden base.

Coypu

Myocaster coypus

Coypus, also known as river rats, are large rodents. They weigh up to 15 kg and reach 64 cm in length. The tail is round, 30–45 cm long and almost hairless. The fur is golden brown on the upper side and grey on the underside. The female has nipples towards the side of her body, so the young can be nursed while swimming.

Coypus have long whiskers on the snout and large reddish brown front teeth. They usually live in fresh water (lakes and streams) but can also survive in brackish water.

Coypus live in large family groups and are often active during the day. They dig long tunnels in embankments and may undermine dykes and dams. The entrances are above water and about 25 cm in diameter.

Coypus were introduced into Europe from South America by fur farmers at the beginning of the twentieth century. Released and escaped animals from fur farms have created well-established populations in many areas of Europe.

Coypus have five toes, with long claws on the front feet. The footprint is about 6 cm long and 6 cm wide. The hind foot has narrow webbing between the toes, and the toes are endowed with stiff hairs to aid swimming, making the prints appear wider. The

The Coypu is active during the day and not particularly shy. Biopix.

tracks of the hind feet are about 12 cm long and 7 cm wide. When the animal moves on soft terrain, you can often detect the tail in the form of serpentine drag marks.

Coypus feed almost exclusively on plants but may also consume insect larvae, mussels, snails, and crustaceans.

Near the burrow and feeding sites by water, the vegetation will be chewed off or heavily trampled. The animals also create visible paths between trails.

Coypu scat is 5–7 cm long, brown and sausage-shaped, and about 1 cm thick. Scat is left everywhere, both in the water and on the shore.

Coypu scat. L-HO.

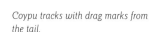

Coypu tracks with drag marks from the tail.

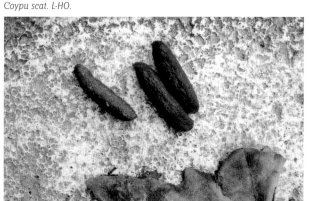

Muskrats are often visible during the day. BPO.

Muskrat

Ondatra zibethicus

Muskrats are large rodents, about 24–40 cm long, with a powerful, compact and scaly tail 19–27.5 cm long. The Muskrat weighs 0.6–1.8 kg. Dry fur is golden brown above and greyish below.

Muskrats live near water, especially fresh water ponds, pools, lakes, canals, and slow-flowing streams and rivers, but can also be found in brackish water with plentiful vegetation. Muskrats live in family groups, and a couple with offspring will hold a clearly established territory.

Muskrats dig tunnels in embankments and build lodges that resemble those of beavers but are smaller and lack tree branches. The entrance is below water level. The underground tunnels of Muskrats can eventually completely undermine dykes and dams.

Muskrats build lodges resembling those built by beavers. PB.

The animals feed on aquatic plants, especially horsetails, reeds, sedges, and grass, but may also consume snails, crustaceans, and especially mussels. They will also feed on fish left behind by Otters. In winter they eat rhizomes and plant roots. In central Europe the Muskrat also eats crops in gardens and fields.

Muskrats are most active early in the morning and at dusk, but they can be seen anytime during the day if they are not disturbed.

Muskrats were introduced into Europe from North America for the fur trade at the beginning of the twentieth century. In Finland, more than 2,000 individuals were released, and today the animals can be found throughout the country. From Finland they have spread to northern Norway and Sweden. In the rest of Europe, animals that have escaped from fur farms have also established themselves in wild populations in many areas. Around the late 1990s or early 2000s, Muskrats from Germany reached Denmark, and this mammal is now spreading further north.

The Muskrat has five toes with long, sharp claws on both front and hind feet. The little toe on the front foot is so small, you often see the impression of only four

A 'Muskrat highway' on a lake shore. TT.

toes. The front footprint is 3–3.5 cm long and about 3.5 cm wide. The hind feet have narrow webbing between the toes, and the toes are equipped with stiff hairs that help in swimming and make the print appear wider. The hind footprint is 5–7 cm long and about 5–6 cm wide. On soft terrain, you can often see drag marks of the tail.

Muskrats live along slow-flowing water or by lakes that do not freeze over. They dig long tunnels in river and stream banks and along shorelines. The entrances are always below water level and 15–20 cm

145

in diameter. The tunnels can be up to 6 m long before reaching the actual living quarters.

On calm water, structures might also be built on a floating wooden base. The buildings, resembling small beaver lodges, are constructed from bulrushes, reeds, grass, and earth, and may reach 1.5 m across and a height of 1 m. The entrance is always below water level.

The Muskrat's scat is dark brown, cylindrical, 1.2 cm wide and about 6 mm thick. In spring it is deposited in mounds on clumps of grass, stones, uprooted or felled trees, tree stumps, etc. The animals may also build mounds with mud and plants and use their scat as a territorial marker; otherwise, you usually see scat in water.

Muskrats also occasionally build nests in an undisturbed place among aquatic plants, where the water is calm.

The Muskrat leaves noticeable tracks in vegetation. On the shore, you come across paths running among plants, and in large, flat, grazed areas you might see chewed-off plant remains in the water. Muskrats will browse a relatively large area.

Muskrats relish river mussels. They press their sharp front teeth into the shells and force the two halves apart. Empty mussel shells prized apart in this manner are easy to find.

Muskrat paths in a marsh.

Northern Water Vole

Arvicola terrestris

Northern Water Voles feel comfortable in the water, but they can often be found in gardens and parks where there are plentiful food supplies. ITL.

Northern Water Voles are also called Water Rats, but these rodents are placed in the extensive vole family. They are 12–26 cm long, but the tail, at 5.5–10.5 cm in length, accounts for more than two-thirds of the total length. They weigh 80–380 g. The Northern Water Vole may live near fresh water or in an entirely dry area, or even change seasonal locations—near water in summer, and in a dry habitat in winter; however, you normally find this vole near water. As its names suggests, Northern Water Vole is an excellent swimmer and will dive under in a flash if it feels threatened.

It is drab in colour, with short legs, small eyes, and short ears. The fur is dark brown or black on the upper body and golden brown underneath. The tail is shorter than that of a rat and has short, protruding hairs.

Northern Water Vole is almost exclusively vegetarian, and reeds, cattails, common rushes, juicy grasses, and herbaceous plants are the preferred diet near water, while in dry areas in summer it eats the exposed parts of plants, including, in winter, the roots of trees and herbs, various flower bulbs, tubers such as potatoes and Jerusalem artichokes, as well as the roots of wild rye and carrots. Turnips are hollowed out from below so only a thin shell remains above ground. In autumn, plentiful supplies are brought into the tunnel

footprints are more than twice the size.

On the shores of lakes and streams, the vole digs tunnels in embankments. Often the plants around the entrance are heavily grazed, and you will find a path about 5 cm wide in the vegetation. By streams and lakes with rich vegetation such as duckweed, you can see their paths leading into the water. On land, the water vole digs large tunnels in the earth and, like a mole, leaves hills behind. If the vole cannot dig its tunnels by pushing the earth through them, it transports earth above ground. Northern Water Vole mounds do not lie in a row or in an organised system like those of a Common Mole, and also are not as large or regular. Close by, but not in the mound itself, you can see an air hole, about 6–8 cm in diameter. Plants are usually completely removed from around the mound.

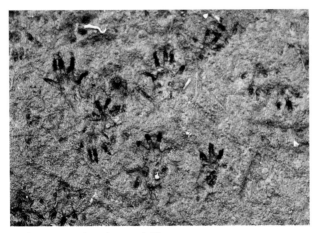

Northern Water Vole tracks in mud. PB.

system, and in winter the bark of trees might also be collected and consumed, especially bark of fruit trees such as apple, plum, and pear.

Each female lives in a clearly established territory, while the male's territory can overlap those of several females.

The vole has four toes on the forefoot. The footprint is about 1.8 cm long and 2.3 cm wide. The hind foot has five toes and is about 3 cm wide. Rats leave similar tracks, but with a somewhat more elongated print on the hind foot, and Muskrat

Near water, the voles transport plants to special feeding sites, where uneaten plant remains are left in heaps. Scent

An entrance hole in an embankment. Biopix.

A Northern Water Vole. LG.

markings are also left here, and there will always be scat.

The scat is cylindrical, greenish to dark brown with rounded ends, 7–10 mm long and 3–4 mm thick, also about twice as large as that of Common Voles. The scat is often left in mounds around entrance holes or at feeding sites.

You can find feeding sites under clumps of grass, where the shortest and juiciest shoots have been gnawed. The feeding sites resemble those of Common Voles, but the water vole's gnaw marks are more powerful.

Water vole scat often lies in mounds. LG.

There is no air hole in the mound itself. PB.

A Northern Water Vole. LG.

Northern Water Voles might eat roots across a wide area of ground. The roots of young trees can be gnawed to such an extent that the tree can be uprooted or topple in a storm.

Water Voles cannot climb, but they can gnaw the bark of trees up to a height of about 20 cm, particularly fruit trees, more commonly if the trunk is surrounded by high, thick grass in which they can hide. The tooth marks are 3.5–4 mm wide and leave an obviously rough surface. You will find unconsumed pieces of bark on the ground that can be up to 1 cm wide and bent at one end and have clearly visible tooth marks.

The vole gnaws hazelnuts in the same way as Wood and Yellow-necked Mice. Once the mouse has gnawed a hole in the shell, it sticks its lower front teeth in the hole, and then gnaws the nut from the inside out. The teeth marks make a row of small grooves around the hole.

The water vole has a powerful bite, and the gnawed edge can appear jagged. On nuts with thinner shells, the gnaw marks look more like a natural break. In autumn, water voles will gather quantities of nuts in their tunnels. During the next autumn, the empty shells are taken out to make room for new supplies. The shells might lie in large piles in front of the nest entrance holes.

Turnips gnawed from below. PB.

Southern Water Vole. CF.

Southern Water Vole

Arvicola sapidus
Southern Water Vole resembles Northern Water Vole but is a little larger. It has a somewhat longer tail and a more pointed snout. It can normally be found near running water, but like Northern Water Vole, it is also found inland. The tracks are similar to those of other voles, but are a little larger. Southern Water Voles feed on bark and roots; near water they prefer willows, rushes, and other marsh plants. They will also consume fresh water mussels.

The Water Shrew is always active and practically never rests. SD.

Water Shrew

Neomys fodiens
The Water Shrew, one of Europe's largest shrews, is an insectivore. The shrew is 7–9.5 cm long, with a tail of 4.5–7.5 cm; it weighs 9–23 g.

The Water Shrew has a sharply pointed snout. The upper body is slate grey to shiny black, the dark colouring clearly contrasting with the silver grey to yellowish underbelly.

The Water Shrew often has white hairs around its eyes and on the snout. The ears are hidden in the fur, which is thick and puffed out with air. When the shrew dives, the fur appears silver-white.

The tail is dark above and paler below. The tail may also occasionally be completely dark, but with a light tip. On the tail is a tuft of stiff hairs that help the Water Shrew when swimming. The hind feet have similar hairs.

Water Shrews are most common in fresh water, especially small lakes and running water with lush vegetation on the banks or shoreline, but they may also be found in wet areas in woodland or meadows without direct access to water, and in coastal habitats if good cover is available.

The Water Shrew dives all the way to the bottom once in water, looking for aquatic insects and their larvae as well as crustaceans, worms and snails. This is a small, quick, and furtive animal that also catches small fish, newts, and amphibians often larger than itself. It can secrete a substance from salivary glands below its lower front teeth that disables its prey. The prey is then brought on land and consumed at specific feeding sites.

On land, Water Shrews eat beetles, snails, earthworms, and other invertebrates, and may also consume carrion.

The shrew lives in loose territories it does not defend particularly assiduously. Several shrews may inhabit the same area. Like other shrews, the Water Shrew is active all year-round.

The front feet have five toes, clearly splayed in the footprints. The feet are about 12 mm long and 10 mm wide. The hind feet also have five toes, but they are a little longer, about 14 mm, and 10 mm wide. On very soft terrain, with mud or

The Water Shrew is a good swimmer. Its feet and tail are equipped with surface hair. SD.

A female Water Shrew has two or three litters each year. TS.

and contains the remains of insects. It is up to 8 mm long, 2 mm thick, and can be found wherever the animals are active, but is often hidden.

The shrew builds a small round nest of leaves, moss, and grass stalks right on the ground. The stalks are dragged into the nest to anchor it well. The nest has only one entrance.

silt, you might also make out the tail print, appearing as a serpentine band. When it jumps, a Water Shrew lands on its front feet first. The two sets of prints can be 4.5 cm apart or even greater.

Water Shrew scat is very small and, with its sharply pointed ends, resembles caraway seeds. The scat is always black

Water Shrews leave very small pathways in the vegetation by water in an area stretching 10 m in each direction from the nest. On land the shrew also leaves small pathways radiating from the nest. In embankments, tunnels with entrances above and below water level may be built. With some luck, right by the shore, you might make out a shrew's feeding sites, and find the remains of its prey.

The Water Shrew eagerly uses its keen sense of smell, and it can consume a little more than its own body weight each day. MLA.

Otter

Lutra lutra

The Otter is a predator and always found near water, usually fresh water; hence, it can easily be confused with European Mink, which lives in the same habitats. The mink, however, is smaller and has a more pointed snout. The Otter's body is streamlined, with a long, muscular tail. When an Otter is swimming, most of its body is beneath the water, but a mink swims considerably higher in the water. An Otter's head is flat with a broad snout, long stiff whiskers, and small round ears.

The fur is brown, lighter below, and the Otter has a light brown neck and cheeks. A European Mink is brown-black and not discernibly lighter on the underparts. The Otter is about 60–80 cm long; the female weighs 5–8 kg, the male 6–12 kg. The tail is 35–45 cm long, about one-third the animal's total length.

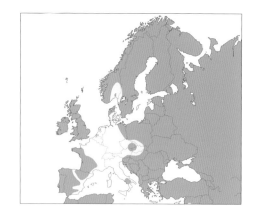

An Otter's legs are short, with wide feet. The Otter swims fast, faster than beavers, muskrats, and water voles. It can dive for up to six minutes, but usually stays under water for no longer than one minute.

The Otter is solitary within its territory. The female's territory is smaller than that of the male, and the latter might overlap that of several females. Males and females

In the winter, after the ice has formed, the Otter needs to find open water to hunt. SS.

are found together only during mating season in spring.

The Otter is nocturnal throughout the year. During the day, it usually hides in hollows in embankments, under the roots of trees, and in other protected places. In coastal areas, however, it may also be active during the day.

The Otter has five webbed toes on each foot. The front footprint is elongated, often traces of the heel are also visible, and the full print is 7–9 cm long, the width about 6 cm. The hind footprint is almost circular, with a diameter of 5–7 cm. The webbing may not be noticeable, and the thumb is also rarely visible. The claws are very small and seen as small points in front of the toe-pad prints.

The Otter normally does not walk with a measured gait, but moves in a bouncy fashion. When the animal is moving at a normal pace, the distance between

An Otter track with clear drag marks from the tail. SJ.

the groups of prints is about 40–80 cm. In snow or in soft mud, you can also see marks left by the dragged tail.

Otters are lively animals. On steep embankments they often create deep ruts

An Otter's glide-path in the snow. AL.

Otter tracks in snow with a wide rut left by belly and tail. PB.

An Otter's feeding site, with empty mussel shells. HP.

Scat is used for territorial marking in dry vegetation. ET.

they use as glide-paths as they slide down the slope. In winter, these can be clearly visible in snow.

Otters feed mostly on fish about 10–15 cm long but may also consume crustaceans, small birds, and large insect larvae in the water, as well as mice and voles on land.

Small fish are consumed in the water, larger ones at feeding sites on land. At

An Otter consumes larger fish, here a wolf fish, on land. SS.

these spots you might also find the remains of meals, which are, however, often quickly eaten by other animals.

Otters scent-mark their territories with scat that is tarry and black and smells strongly of fish. The smell is slightly sweet and not so unpleasant as that of mink scat. Older scat is greyish and crumbles easily. The scat contains fish scales and bones, as well as the remains of crabs and insects, and is often left on stones or in clumps of grass.

American Mink

Mustela vison

The American Mink was introduced into Europe from North America in the early 1900s for fur farming. Escapes from farms have now established widespread wild populations in Europe.

The American Mink is approximately the size of a Western Polecat, about 30–47 cm long, with a tail measuring 13–23 cm. The male weighs 1–1.5 kg; the female is significantly smaller and rarely weighs more than 0.8 kg.

American Mink from fur farms can be a variety of colours, ranging from white to bluish black, while wild animals are normally dark brown with white spots on the lower lip and throat. They are almost never light coloured on the snout.

The American Mink is a good swimmer and prefers living near water, both in fresh water environments and in coastal areas, wherever there are stones, rocks, or marsh, which helps provide cover, but it will also utilise drier habitats. It is normally nocturnal, but may sometimes be seen during the day, and it can sometimes be found in harbours and other man-made habitats.

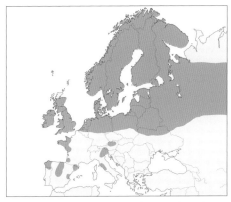

The American Mink is less inclined to dig a den than Western Polecat, but prefers to sleep under tree roots, in hollow trees, under harbour piers, in sheds or boats, as well as on the beach, hidden between rocks, or simply in taller vegetation near the water.

The tracks resemble those of Western Polecat. They are somewhat smaller, but the differences aren't easy to see—except for the fact that the mink often moves along shorelines when looking for food. The claws of Western Polecat are longer, especially on the front feet, and often leave a clearer print.

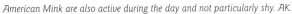

American Mink are also active during the day and not particularly shy. AK.

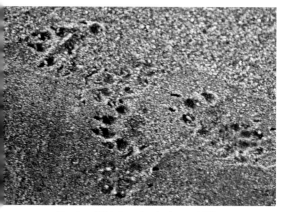

American Mink footprints in the sand. AK.

The American Mink has five toes on each foot. The front footprints are about 3 cm long and 4 cm wide. The feet have narrow webbing between the toes that is visible now and then in the print. The length of the stride is about 40–90 cm.

The gait of the American Mink resembles that of Western Polecat, but the mink moves more lightly in deep snow. It travels in a straight line for long stretches when not foraging for food, even in snow. It can forage under snow or suddenly disappear into a hole in the ice when prey is detected. You can find mink tracks along shores with soft sand or mud; when the prints are clear, the dragged tail will leave a visible track.

American Mink feed mostly on fish and crustaceans but also hunt small mammals, birds, amphibians, crabs, and insects. They also hunt small ducks and can kill game birds. The scat is similar to that of Western Polecat and is cylindrical, slightly twisted, with a long point at one end, and 5–10 cm long and about 1 cm thick. It can often be identified because of its dark colour and the obvious remains of fish scales and bones. If the scat contains copious fish remains, it becomes loose and can easily crumble. Fresh scat has a strong sulphurous musty smell. The scat is not always left in latrines and is often visible on stones, tree stumps,

Paired footprints of an American Mink. OJ.

American Mink scat. KR.

Fish scales and fins, among other items, may be found at a mink's feeding site. EHA.

bridges, etc. Otter scat has a sweeter smell than that of American Mink.

The American Mink prefers eating its prey in secluded areas, and if you happen upon such a place, you will always see remains, typically of crabs, prawns, fish, eggshells, etc.

American Minks will kill a wide range of prey, including voles and ducks. HS.

European Mink. VS.

European Mink

Mustela lutreola

The European Mink resembles American Mink and Western Polecat. It is dark brown with narrow white patches around the snout, with variable white areas on the throat and chest and a dark undercoat. The European Mink is also smaller than American Mink and Western Polecat.

European Mink is usually found near water, in reed beds and swampy areas near woodland. The behaviour and habits of European Mink are similar to those of its American cousin. European Mink swims and dives exceedingly well and lives primarily on fish, crabs, amphibians, small birds, and small mammals.

It builds its nest between tree roots, among reeds, in hollow trees, or in a den, which it usually excavates in an embankment. The entrance is above water level. European Mink has webbing between its five toes, and this can be seen occasionally in footprints on soft terrain; otherwise, the tracks resemble those of American Mink.

European Mink. Bioecologie.

Western Polecat

Mustela putorius

Western Polecat is a small marten. The female is 29–37 cm long, with a tail of about 11–17 cm. The male is larger, 35–46 cm long, with a tail of about 13–19 cm; the female weighs 0.5–0.8 kg, the male, 0.7–1.5 kg.

The area around the snout is white, with black around the eyes; behind the eyes there is a variably sized white patch reaching from the face to under the ears. The ears are dark with white tips. The undercoat is light grey or yellowish; the coat is black. The belly and legs are dark. The coat is darker in summer than in winter.

Western Polecats live in deciduous and mixed woodland, preferably near water or wetland areas, but may also inhabit damp meadows and cultivated areas that are not farmed too intensively. They are also found in dry areas with Rabbit colonies. Polecats may also live in urban areas. Western Polecats don't like to climb, so if they inhabit buildings, they are normally found at ground level. They are nocturnal but may sometimes be seen during the day.

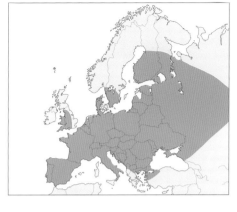

Western Polecats establish territories, but males and females are both solitary, except during mating season. They do not hibernate, but are not as active in winter as in summer. They have five toes with long claws on both front and hind feet. The front footprint is 3–3.5 cm long and 2.5–4 cm wide. The prints of the hind feet are about 4.5 cm long and 4 cm wide. Since polecats normally jump-walk, you almost always see two parallel sets of tracks; in snow and on soft terrain, tail tracks might be visible. The prints resemble those of an American Mink, and the length of the stride is 40–60 cm.

A Western Polecat at the entrance to its den. LG.

Scat of Western Polecat. Biopix.

Tracks of a Western Polecat, with the tail track clearly visible. PB.

Western Polecats feed principally on amphibians and Rabbits, but they also catch snakes, mice, and rats. They may also consume small fish and insects, birds, and eggs, as well as carrion.

Their scat is dark, 5–8 cm long and 0.5–1 cm thick, and twisted and pointed at one end. The scat contains hair and bones, but normally no fish bones or

Western Polecat is nocturnal and rarely active during the day. LG.

scales. The scat smells very strong and has an unpleasant odour, but it is not used to scent-mark territory. The scat is often left in mounds in latrines near the den. When polecats go on poultry raids, they remove eggs to take to a spot where they can eat them without disturbance.

In wetter areas you might find plentiful remains of frogs and toads, especially toad heads at feeding sites; apparently polecats leave the toad heads to avoid their poison glands.

Western Polecats utilise a variety of cavities, living, for example, in Rabbit burrows and old fox dens, under tree roots, in hollow trees, as well as in sheds and even under abandoned cars. If adequate nest sites cannot be found, the polecat digs a den in a dry embankment, especially near a stream or river.

Pine Marten

Martes martes

The Pine Marten closely resembles Beech Marten. It is reddish or chocolate brown, with a yellowish to orange area on its chest. This pale area is solid and does not continue to the front feet as it does on Beech Marten. The Pine Marten is slimmer and somewhat more long-legged than Beech Marten, at about 15 cm high at the shoulder, and has more pointed ears. The Pine Marten's snout is dark.

Pine Marten is 36–65 cm long, with a 20–25 cm tail; the female weighs 0.7–1.2 kg, the male 1.3–1.8 kg.

Pine Martens live in mature mixed or conifer woodland with clearings, especially woodland with plenty of dead and old hollow trees, but they might also be found in sheds and barns in agricultural areas. Pine Martens are nocturnal, but in northern Scandinavia, when the days are long, they can also be seen during the day, mainly just before dusk. During the day, martens sleep in abandoned squirrel or raptor nests, in hollow trees, or between rocks.

Pine Martens feed on small rodents and birds; occasionally they also take pigeons

and poultry. They can also catch squirrels in treetops, and will eat berries and fruit in the summer. Pine Martens will also eat grass. The scat is similar to that of Beech Marten, and can also resemble that of a fox, but the scat of Pine Marten is often smaller and smells similar to the musk of deer. The scat is 8–10 cm long, 1–1.2 cm thick, somewhat twisted and usually pointed at one end; it is normally black and contains the remains of hair and feathers. Scat is left in the open on stones, clumps of grass, and tree stumps, but it is especially abundant on trees in which the Pine Marten rests during the day.

Pine Martens climb so well, they can catch squirrels in the treetops. Note the yellow area on this marten's neck. LG.

Pine Marten tracks are similar to those of Beech Marten, but since Pine Martens have more hair on their feet, the prints in snow may appear larger and more blurred. The tracks might also resemble those of hares, though a marten's tracks are often located right below or very close to a tree; the marten also has five toes on each foot, whereas hares have only four.

The front footprint, not including the heel, is 3.5–5 cm long and about 3.5 cm wide. The hind footprint is somewhat smaller, 3–3.5 cm long and about 3 cm wide.

Like most martens, Pine Marten jump-walks, and the length between front and hind foot is 50–80 cm.

Pine Marten scat. JH; inset, ED.

Pine Marten tracks in snow. Left, LGA; right, LG.

Beech Marten
Martes foina

Beech Marten has dark fur with a grey-ish white undercoat. It has a white patch on its throat that divides on the chest and reaches all the way to the inside of the front legs. The snout is light brown. The patch on the chest of a Pine Marten may be yellow or orange and is solid, and it does not extend to the front legs.

Beech Marten is about 42–48 cm long; the tail measures 23–26 cm, and the height at the shoulder is about 12 cm; the female weighs 0.9–1.9 kg, the male 1.3–2.3 kg.

Beech Martens live in small areas of woodland, in farmyards, or in open land-scapes with abundant rodents and small birds; they can also be found in campsites and on the periphery of residential areas. In southern Europe they also occur in rocky and mountainous areas.

Beech Martens are territorial and noc-turnal, and during the day they rest in old squirrel or raptor nests, hollow trees, or old fox dens, between large stones or rocks, or in wood piles, sheds, barns, or other farm buildings.

The Beech Marten has five toes, but the inner toe print is often not visible. The

Beech Marten has a white patch on its neck. LG.

Beech Marten tracks. LG.

The scat is sausage-shaped, clumped, and pointed at the ends, 8–10 cm long and 1.2–1.5 cm thick. It contains hair, feathers, and bones, and in summer and autumn might also contain the stones of fruit. When fresh, it is pungent. The scat can be found on paths, but it is usually found in piles or in latrines close to the diurnal sleeping quarters.

In a Beech Marten's territory, you will happen across the remains of prey, especially birds, but also eggshells and hedgehogs—completely consumed except for the quills and skin. The eggshells show small holes, and these are marten tooth marks left after one or more eggs have been carried in the marten's mouth. After the Beech Marten has bitten a hole in an egg, it presses its snout inside and licks out the contents. This is why the edges of such eggshells are usually bent inward.

front footprints are larger than the hind. The prints can often be seen in pairs, and these are always the paired prints of front or hind feet. When the animal is jump-walking, the prints might resemble those of a hare; in other words, the hind footprints are set obliquely to each other, and the front footprints are somewhat longer.

The tracks clearly show claw marks. The front footprints are about 3.5 cm long and 3.2 cm wide; the hind footprints are smaller, about 3 cm long and 2.5 cm wide. The stride is about 30–50 cm.

It is almost impossible to separate the tracks of a Beech Marten from those of a Pine Marten, although the latter are a little larger and often more blurred.

Beech Martens feed on small rodents, especially Common Voles, also rats and small birds. Also on the Beech Marten menu are Western Hedgehogs, moles, young squirrels, pigeons, poultry, ducks, raptors, owls, and birds' eggs, as well as large insects and fruit such as cherries, gooseberries, and plums.

Beech Marten scat.

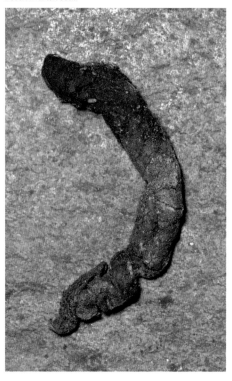

Stoat

Mustela erminea

The Stoat is sometimes called a Short-tailed Weasel. It is a very small, slender and nimble animal, about the size of a rat. The female is 16–22 cm long, the male 23–29 cm. The female's tail measures 7–8 cm, the male's 9–10 cm; the female weighs 80–150 g, and the male is about twice as heavy, 150–300 g.

In summer the Stoat is yellowish brown above and white below. The colours are clearly separated; the tail is 4–5 cm long with a black tip. In northern Europe, the Stoat has a white coat in winter, though still with the black tip to its tail; but this colour change does not occur in the rest of Europe.

The Stoat prefers areas with tall grass, such as meadows and open fields near woodland, broad hedgerows, and stone walls, also areas near Rabbit colonies. Stoats can also be found in inhabited areas in wood or stone piles, under porches, in roomy cellars, or in sheds and barns.

The Stoat is territorial and active both day and night. It does not dig its own den but instead lives in a variety of natural cavities that can be cushioned with the hair of its prey.

A Stoat in its summer coat. AK.

The Stoat's tracks are very small and closely resemble those of Western Polecat and American Mink. The tracks are most visible in snow, where they can be seen in paired rows together with marks of the animal's body. The track sequence is never entirely straight over longer stretches, since Stoats always jump around when hunting and may also disappear under the snow, between stones, rocks, or tree roots, and into other cavities. Occasionally you can see clear hind footprints, and this is where the animal stood upright to scan territory. The length of a Stoat's jump is 30–70 cm.

A Stoat with a Northern Water Vole. SS.

In northern Europe, the fur of Stoats changes to a white winter coat. AK.

The Stoat has five toes on each foot. The front footprints are about 2 cm long and 1.5 cm wide, the hind footprint, 3.5–4 cm long and about 1.5 cm wide, and tracks are very similar to those of a Weasel.

Stoats feed primarily on small rodents and Northern Water Voles, but also eat the young and eggs of small birds, young hares, Rabbits, and small game birds. The prey is killed with a bite to the neck. The Stoat often drags its prey to a secure feeding site where you can find remnants of the meal. It also caches small amounts of food left from its meals. The Stoat's scat is 4–8 cm long and about 0.5 cm thick,

A Stoat's tracks in snow. Left, LG; above, AK.

greyish brown to black, twisted, clumpy, and pointed at one end. The scat contains hair and other remains and smells pungent when fresh. Scat is often left in plain sight in prominent locations.

Weasel

Mustela nivalis

The Weasel is the smallest predator in Europe. In northern and eastern Europe, Weasels are very small; the female is 11–15 cm long and weighs 20–40 g, and the male is 15–19.5 cm long, weighing 40–80 g. In the rest of Europe the female can reach lengths of 19 cm and weigh up to 75 g, the male up to 23 cm in length and up to 130 g in weight—in other words, about the size of a female Stoat. The tail is 3–5 cm long and uniformly brown, without the black tip of a Stoat.

The Weasel is reddish brown above, greyish white below. The northern populations have a clear colour demarcation, whereas in southern populations, the transition is not uniform, and brown spots might appear on the white underside. The Weasel changes colour in the north; in the south it maintains the same colour year-round.

Weasels frequent the same habitats as Stoat, including woodland edges, broad field edges, hedgerows, stone walls, underbrush, clearings in woodland, and moorland and meadows. Weasels can also be seen near buildings, and are found between floors and in cellars. They are active day and night in their territory.

Since Stoats hunt the same prey as Weasels, they will often chase a Weasel out of their territory; as a result, you will not regularly find the tracks of both animals in the same spot. Weasel tracks are similar to those of Stoat but smaller. The prints are 1–1.5 cm long, and about 1 cm wide. When a Weasel moves in snow, the tracks of its whole body are visible, and traces of the prey's blood might also be seen. Normally, however, Weasels move underneath the snow, or in the tunnels of small rodents or moles, and this is the reason the tracks are often not seen. The jump-stride is 20–70 cm.

The Weasel is so small, it can hunt mice in their own tunnels. HS.

The Weasel feeds primarily on small rodents and prefers slow-moving voles. Weasels, especially females, will pursue rodents in the rodents' own tunnels. The somewhat larger males are too large for this but can kill Rabbits in their burrows. Weasels are excellent climbers and take birds from trees and nest boxes. When dealing with large eggs, the Weasel will start by biting a hole in the upper part of the egg, in the same manner as a Stoat. Prey is usually killed with a single bite to the neck. When a Weasel has killed more prey than it can eat, it caches the food, often close to the burrow. Its scat is grey-ish brown to black, twisted, and pointed. Scat is 2–5 cm long, 2–3 mm thick, and can often be found near resting areas and food caches.

A Weasel with brown spots on its cheeks. LG.

A Weasel has entered a mouse's tunnel under the snow. JK.

Brown Hare

Lepus europaeus

The Brown Hare is dark brown above, light yellow-brown on its sides, and white on the belly. The ears are black-tipped, and the iris is light yellow. Brown Hare is about 55–70 cm long, and the tail, which measures about 10 cm, is black above and white below. It weighs 3.5–7 kg, with the female slightly larger than the male. You can find hares in all habitats, except for extensive areas of woodland.

Hares are common in open farmland near woods, hedges, and underbrush. They are mostly solitary and particularly active in the evening and at night, but in the mating season you can see small groups in fields even during the day.

Brown Hares have five toes on the front feet, but the innermost toe is so short that its imprint is only rarely visible. The hind foot is long and narrow and has four toes. All toes have narrow straight claws that are clearly visible in the tracks. Hares have no visible pads on their feet; instead, the soles are covered with a thick, insulating, feathery layer of hair. In the middle of the foot, this layer is particularly thick, getting sparser towards the front. This hair ensures the animal doesn't fall over on

Brown Hare. AK.

Brown Hare tracks in mud. Note the hair marks on the sole of the foot. PB.

Track of a Brown Hare, with the front feet behind the larger hind feet as the animal runs. LM.

smooth and slippery surfaces. The front footprint is 5–6 cm long and 3 cm wide; the hind footprints are 6–12 cm long and about 3.5 cm wide.

Hares normally move by hopping. They place one front leg immediately behind the other, in an almost straight line, in the direction they are moving, then swing the hind legs forward, around the front legs. The hind legs land almost simultaneously and leave two larger and longer marks ahead of the front feet, almost exactly one set of prints directly in front of the other. The faster the hare runs, the greater the distance between the tracks of the hind and front legs, as well as between groups of

Brown Hares place their hind legs in front of their front legs when moving. Left, LG; right, Biopix.

prints. At very high speeds, the hind footprints may be slightly offset.

Brown Hares will follow the same trail
for large distances, creating trails with
trampled earth and vegetation as a result.
Several hares might use the same trails,
and the trails might also be used by other
animals, including deer.

Hares often turn around and partially
retrace their steps, then jump to one side
and move in a completely different direction. This is particularly common when
they are being pursued, and these sideways
jumps allow them to change direction—
by as much as 90 degrees—without los-
ing speed. Over short distances, hares can
reach speeds of up to 80 km per hour and
jump up to 2.5 m.

When hares sit, they leave the long prints
of the hind legs next to those of the front.
During the day, hares often rest in depressions in the earth, called 'forms', which they
create by scraping away vegetation with
their feet. The form is usually long, and
deep and wide towards the back end. You
usually find clumps of grass or stones by the
form, which provide a measure of protec-
tion for the resting animal. Hares sit with
their hindquarters inside the form, with the
hind legs tucked under the body and the
front legs fully stretched out in front.

Hares are herbivores. In summer they
eat succulent green plants, in winter a
variety of fruits, particularly rose hips and
hawthorn berries, but they may also eat
turnips and the branches and bark of small
trees, especially fruit trees. Their gnaw
marks on trunks are deep and powerful.
Trees that have been browsed in this fashion may, in time, be reduced to the size of
dwarf bushes. Branches are bitten off with
one smooth, oblique cut, as if by a knife.

The hare's pill-shaped scat is oval and
slightly flattened, with a diameter of
12–20 mm. Remains of their plant diet are
easily recognisable in the scat, especially
in winter. In winter the scat is light brown

A Brown Hare's winter scat. LG.

and very dry; in summer it is softer and
darker. The scat can be almost completely
black, and slightly pointed at one end. Unlike Rabbits, hares rarely use latrines, and
scat can normally be found in areas where
the animals eat. In these places you might
see small mounds of scat, but hares also
leave individual droppings in their tracks.

The Brown Hare's large and visible 'form'. AT.

Mountain Hare is brown year-round in the southern part of its range, with a coat similar to the summer coat of individuals in the northernmost parts of the range. AK.

Mountain Hare

Lepus timidus

Mountain Hare is somewhat smaller than Brown Hare, 45–60 cm long with a tail measuring 5–7 cm; it weighs 2–4 kg, females being larger than males. The coat is greyish brown above, lighter on the sides, and white on the belly. The ears are black-tipped, like those of Brown Hare, but the tail is completely white. In northern Scandinavia and in montane environments, Mountain Hares have a white winter coat but retain the black tips to the ears. The iris is a dark reddish brown.

Mountain Hares prefer coniferous forest with underbrush or a scattering of deciduous trees and bushes, and are only rarely found in open fields.

Mountain Hare scat and gnaw marks resemble those of Brown Hare, so it is

A Mountain Hare in its winter coat in a snow form. If a hare is threatened, it can run extremely fast to avoid a predator. AK.

difficult to distinguish these species where both occur; however, you don't usually see scat near the daytime rest site of a Mountain Hare.

On firm ground, it is practically impossible to tell the footprints of Alpine from those of Mountain Hares, but in snow the print of a Mountain Hare's hind foot is somewhat broader, since it can splay its toes to form a snowshoe, which is why it moves more easily in snow than a Brown Hare. Additionally, Mountain Hare is lighter than Brown, therefore it sinks into the snow less easily. The front footprints are 5–7 cm long, the hind 7–10 cm.

Mountain Hares are active in snow, and in summer you might find feeding marks on vegetation at the maximum height of the previous winter's snow. Mountain Hares gnaw horizontally across a trunk, whereas deer gnaw vertically. A Mountain Hare's tooth marks are much less visible.

Hares sever the branches of small trees and bushes with a smooth cut, while deer normally twist branches off, fraying the branch at the point of separation. In deep snow, Mountain Hares often dig short, vaulted tunnels next to the form to serve as escape routes where the animal can quickly hide.

Typical tracks of a Mountain Hare. AK.

Rabbit

Oryctolagus cuniculus

Rabbits are smaller than hares. Males and females are the same size, each about 34–50 cm long, and the tail measures 5 cm and is black above with a distinct white underside. When the Rabbit runs, it raises its tail, and the white underside is clearly visible. The ears lack the black tip found on the ears of hares. Rabbits weigh about 1.5–2.5 kg. Compared with hares, Rabbits have more powerful front legs and shorter hind legs.

Rabbits feed exclusively on plants. They are social animals and live in colonies. They can be active both day and night, but you see them mostly in the morning and at dusk.

Rabbits have five toes on their front feet, but the innermost toe does not leave a print. The other claws leave clear marks. From their prints, Rabbits appear to have no toe pads; instead, the soles of their feet are covered with a thick, insulating, feathery layer of hair like that of hares.

The front footprint is 3–4 cm long and about 2.5 cm wide, the hind footprint, 4–7 cm long and about 2.5 cm wide.

Rabbits were introduced into many European countries. Biopix.

Like hares, Rabbits move in a hopping gait. They set their front legs down first, one directly behind the other in an almost straight line in the direction of movement. Then they rotate the hind legs forward, around and in front of the forelegs. The back legs land almost simultaneously, leaving two larger and more elongated tracks ahead of the forefeet and almost immediately one in front of the other. The length of the stride is 20–50 cm. The faster the animal moves, the greater the distance between front and hind legs. Since Rabbits have shorter hind legs than hares, they cannot jump as far, so the distance between the groups of tracks is 80 cm at most.

Rabbit colonies are easily recognisable in both summer and winter because of their clearly marked trails.

Rabbits dig an underground system of tunnels, usually where the ground will remain relatively dry even when it rains. You often find these tunnels in dry and light soil, especially on slopes, in embankments, on hills, and in dykes near hedges and bushes, or at woodland edges. New colonies may also be established at the edges of fields, comprising only one or a few holes.

Rabbits dig with their front feet and shove the earth away with their hind legs.

The entrance is about 10–30 cm in diameter, but occasionally can measure up to 0.5 m. From the entrance, the tunnel might stretch for several metres underground and connect to other tunnels in a network with numerous entrances. In this system of tunnels, the Rabbit can access smaller areas where it can take cover in bad weather or when in danger.

The entrance to a tunnel is often dug from the outside, and this is why you will find excavated, trampled earth in front of the hole; but the hole can also be dug from the inside, and in this case you will

The entrances to burrows are obvious. You will also find scat in small piles here. KR.

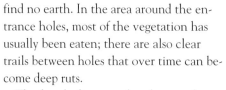

Rabbit scat in a latrine. LG.

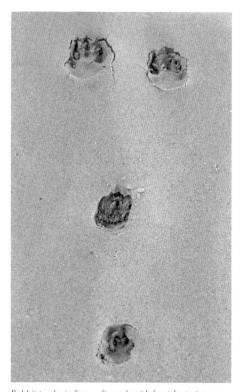

Rabbit tracks in fine, soft sand, with front footprint below, hind footprint above. LG.

find no earth. In the area around the entrance holes, most of the vegetation has usually been eaten; there are also clear trails between holes that over time can become deep ruts.

The female digs nest chambers, cushioned with grass and hair. When she leaves the nest, she covers the entrance with earth mixed with urine and scat. A covered entrance hole might be a sign that newborns are inside.

Rabbit trails are not as long as those used by hares, because Rabbits don't move as far away from their colonies. The trails are often heavily trampled and grazed completely bare.

The scat is 0.7–1 cm in diameter; when compared with a hare's, it is quite spherical. It is almost black or greenish, but bleaches with time; after about three weeks it is a uniform brown.

In a colony, Rabbits use established latrines which form large mounds; however, scat is also visible in prominent places such as in clumps of grass, on tree stumps, on mole hills, and in depressions, as well as along trails and near entrances to the tunnels, often as a way to mark territory.

Rabbits have the same chisel-shaped teeth as hares, with 2 isolated teeth in the upper jaw. Gnaw marks on trees and bushes often look like the work of 4 teeth. Like hares, Rabbits can feed on the bark and branches of small trees up to a height of 60 cm, and you might also find tooth marks on turnips or large mushrooms.

Red Squirrel
Sciurus vulgaris

The Red Squirrel is a rodent about 19–25 cm long. Its bushy tail measures 15–20 cm, and it weighs 200–425 g; the female is larger than the male. The coat is reddish but in the winter turns slightly grey, but in northern Scandinavia it is completely grey in winter. Individuals with a completely black coat also occur. A Red Squirrel has prominent ear tufts that grow larger in the winter.

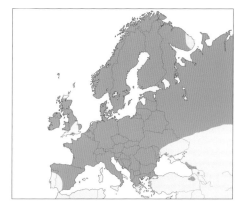

Red Squirrels feed principally on plants, conifer buds, beechnuts, acorns, nuts, and mushrooms as well as fruit and berries but will also take insects and occasionally birds' eggs and young.

Squirrels are active during the day and prefer deciduous or mixed woodland, but they also inhabit gardens and parks. Squirrels are agile climbers; they can turn their hind feet 180 degrees to help climb down a tree headfirst.

The toes are long, narrow, and very dexterous. Squirrels have powerful curved claws and large foot pads. The front foot has five toes, but the thumb is very small and has one flat nail that does not leave a mark. The footprints are 3–4 cm long, and about 2 cm wide, while those of the hind feet are 5–6 cm long and 2.5–3.5 cm wide.

Red Squirrels spend the majority of their time in trees, so their tracks usually begin and end at a tree. On the ground,

A young Red Squirrel in its dark summer coat. AK.

they move in jumps, exactly the way a Rabbit does, placing their front feet first, and then the hind feet in front of them, and this is the reason the prints of the front feet are found close together in the direction of movement. Immediately in front of the front footprints, those of the hind feet leave broader marks, and they are normally slightly oblique. When the squirrel moves normally, the distance between prints is 30–50 cm, but when it runs, the distance can be up to 1 m.

The scat is almost spherical, slightly flattened, and pointed at one end. In summer it is brown, 5–8 mm long and 5–6 mm thick; in winter it is darker or even black and usually smaller. It contains finely ground plant matter and occasionally the indigestible parts of insects. You normally find scat under trees, scattered on the ground, or at feeding sites.

The female builds a spherical nest, called a drey, high up in a tree. Unlike the somewhat larger Magpie nests, squirrel nests are built abutting the trunk, preferably in the fork of a branch. They are commonly found in conifers but can also be in deciduous trees. The drey is built from branches and twigs and then anchored to branches so it is not blown away in a storm. The nest is about the size of a football, about 30–50 cm in diameter, with a lateral entry hole of about 5 cm. The nest is somewhat loose in structure and filled with grass, moss, and strips of bark.

The innermost part of the nest is cushioned with hair, feathers, and other soft materials.

In addition to this nest, squirrels may also resort to other, simpler resting places in their territory, or sleep in hollow trees or large nest boxes.

Red Squirrels will peel bark off trees, and you may find loose bark as a result. Particular favourites are larches, oaks, beeches, birches, and sundry conifers.

Red Squirrel tracks in snow. Below are the tracks of the front feet, above these the prints of the hind feet. AK.

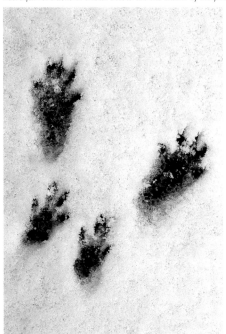

When used to build a nest, bark is not eaten and there are no tooth marks. When squirrels eat part of the softer cambium under the bark of a tree, you can see clear gnaw marks on the tree and bark strewn around.

Squirrels eat the buds and younger branches of conifers, especially spruces. The gnaw marks are uniform. The branches are chewed off directly behind the male flowers, and the buds are hollowed out, leaving a cup-shaped remnant. Large quantities of chewed-off branches often lie below trees.

Fir and pine cones are bitten off. The squirrel holds the cone in its front feet by the tip and chews off the outer scales of the cone to get to the seeds. Cones that have been gnawed on by squirrels have a frayed and somewhat pointed appearance, like a little brush. The base of the cone is always frayed. When cones are gnawed on by mice, the base is always smooth, and mice also leave a smaller point on the cone.

Squirrels eat cones on moss-covered hillocks or tree stumps, where the discarded cones and scales can be found in great numbers. The animals also eat cones up in the trees. They will often use favoured feeding sites, and here you will find the remains of cones on the ground; mice prefer eating in secluded and well-hidden places.

Squirrels hold hazelnuts with their front feet. They gnaw off the tip to form a small opening, then use their lower teeth like a crowbar to gain access to the kernel. They crack open the stones of fruit in the same manner.

Squirrels open walnuts by pressing their lower incisors into the thinner parts of the shell and then using the teeth to prize open the shell.

Squirrels like the grubs in pineapple galls, which can be found on the green

Squirrels hold food with their front feet. AK.

shoots of fir trees. The shoot with the gall is bitten off, and the grub is exposed and consumed.

Red Squirrels eat a lot of mushrooms, and the teeth marks can be seen as

Hazelnuts gnawed on by squirrels. LG.

181

A Red Squirrel with a pine cone. LG.

indentations 4–5 mm wide. Squirrels even store mushrooms to dry, placing them on forks in branches or skewering them on broken branches.

They stock winter supplies of beechnuts, acorns, and hazelnuts, either massed or stuck individually in cracks and crevices in trees or small holes in the ground. When squirrels forget the location of these supplies, young trees sprout from uneaten nuts.

Pine cones gnawed by squirrels are frayed and scattered everywhere, often on stones or mounds. LG.

Grey Squirrel
Neosciurus carolinensis

The Grey Squirrel is a little larger than Red Squirrel, 23–30 cm long, with a tail length of 19–25 cm. It weighs 350–800 g. The ear tufts are much less pronounced than those of Red Squirrel. The fur is normally grey to grey-brown but may also be completely black, though the toes are always grey. Grey Squirrels much prefer deciduous woodland.

While quite similar to Red Squirrels in behaviour, Greys are heavier and not as agile, and they spend more time foraging on the ground. The nest is usually found in a tree hole, but they may build a nest on the fork of a branch, almost always in a deciduous tree.

The tracks are similar to those of Red Squirrel, with virtually no discernible differences.

Grey Squirrels occur naturally in North America. They were introduced into England and Ireland and have largely displaced Red Squirrels there. Biopix.

183

Flying Squirrels do not fly, but thanks to the folds of skin between their front and hind legs, they can glide from tree to tree, using the tail as a rudder. BP.

A Flying Squirrel in its lighter winter coat. NPL.

Flying Squirrel

Pteromys volans

The Flying Squirrel is a small animal, 15–20 cm long, with a tail measuring 9–14 cm. It weighs 95–175 g. The eyes are large, the ears small and without tufts; the coat is silver-grey above and white beneath, the tail is grey. On the sides of the body, Flying Squirrels have a fold of skin; when extended between front and hind legs, it is used to glide from tree to tree. Flying Squirrels are not capable of powered flight but can glide up to 50 m. They are rarely seen on the ground.

Flying Squirrels are nocturnal. They prefer mature, undisturbed mixed woodland, usually where there are plenty of old woodpeckers holes, which are used for nests and for storing flood. Flying Squirrels can also be found in gardens and near houses, where they use nest boxes and man-made cavities.

They feed mostly on buds, young shoots, leaves, seeds, nuts, and berries but can also eat birds' eggs and their young. In winter they eat food they have stockpiled as well as birch and alder catkins and twigs.

Flying Squirrel tracks are different from those of other arboreal squirrels. The hind footprints fall close together behind those of the front feet. The Flying Squirrel can also hop on the ground, without using its front legs; when it does, only the prints of the hind legs are visible.

Birch catkins in a Flying Squirrel's larder. YS.

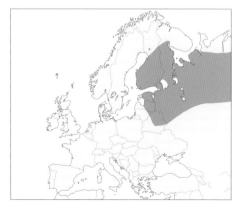

Alpine Marmot

Marmota marmota

Alpine Marmots are large, powerfully built rodents and are members of the squirrel family. They have very short legs and a relatively long, thick tail. They reach 60 cm in length, weigh 2.5–6.5 kg, and have a tail that measures 15–20 cm. The fur is thick and long, with the ears barely visible under the fur. This marmot is greyish brown or greyish black from the head down the back, and a slightly lighter reddish brown on the undersides. The cheeks are slightly paler.

Alpine Marmots are active during the day and feed on grass, herbs, roots, and berries. They live in family groups or larger colonies consisting of 5–15 individuals. One marmot will sit upright on its hind legs and work as a lookout while the other marmots eat. Alpine Marmots dig tunnels in the earth that are up to 10 m long and 3 m deep, where they retreat as soon as they sense a threat. They give loud warning signals at the first sign of danger. With the first frosts, marmots go into hibernation in deep tunnels cushioned with dry grass; the entrance hole is sealed with earth, and the animals will hibernate for up to six months.

Alpine Marmots normally live in grassy embankments in the Alps above tree line and up to an altitude of 3,200 m; they have also been introduced into the Pyrenees, the Apennines, the Vosges, and a variety of countries (Poland, Rumania, Slovakia, and Slovenia among others).

Alpine Marmots can be seen only in the summer. WWE.

Tracks of an Alpine Marmot in snow, the front footprints behind the pair of hind footprints. PB.

The tracks clearly show the small oval prints of the five toes of the hind feet and the four toes of the front. The print of the midsection of the ball of the foot appears as a large single print with wavy borders. The heel leaves two distinct marks, the inner somewhat larger than the outer. The hind footprint is about 5.5 cm long and 4 cm wide; the front footprint is about 5 cm long and 3.5 cm wide.

When walking, a marmot places its hind feet in the prints of the front feet. The stride is normally about 20 cm, but when the marmot scampers, it is about 50

The Alpine Marmot has powerful digging claws on its hind feet. IA.

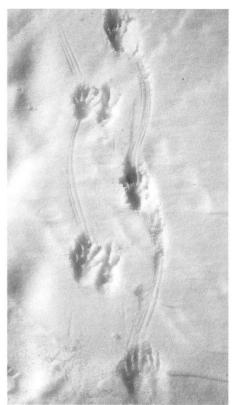

Alpine Marmots have short legs that leave drag marks in the snow. ED.

cm, and the prints of the hind feet fall in front of those of the front feet.

The entrance to the tunnel system is usually in a slope with a southern or southwestern exposure, sometimes also beneath rocks or large stones. The entrance holes are somewhat larger than those made by a Rabbit.

The entrance to an Alpine Marmot's burrow. PB.

A European Souslik carrying building material. KHI.

One of the adults is always on the lookout for predators and warns the family with loud calls. WWE.

European Souslik
Spermophilus citellus

European Souslik is a large rodent with greyish brown upperparts and a lighter underside. It is 19–22 cm long; the tail measures 5.5–7.5 cm and the animal weighs 230–340 g. The prints are small; the front foot has four toes and the tracks are about 1.8 cm long and 1.2 cm wide; the hind foot has five toes, the tracks are about 2 cm long and 1.3 cm wide.

European Sousliks live in large family groups in open grassland, where they are active during the day but spend the night in large underground tunnels. The entrance holes are somewhat smaller than those excavated by Rabbits. Sousliks feed on roots, plant shoots, blossoms, seeds, and berries but also consume insects and other small animals. They hibernate from November to March.

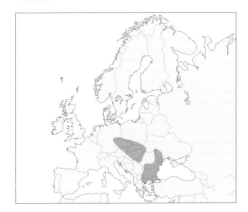

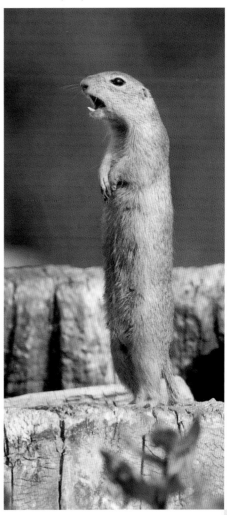

True mice (rodent family Muridae) have long legs and long tails. They have large eyes and ears and normally move in a series of jumps. Their tracks resemble those of squirrels; they place their hind feet next to the footprints of the front. You can often see tracks left by the tail. The scat is usually pointed.

Black Rat

Rattus rattus

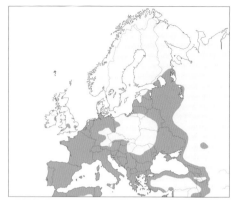

The Black Rat, also known as the Ship Rat, is found close to humans, even more frequently than Brown Rat. Black Rat is often brought by ships to port cities, and then takes up residence in storage buildings, grain and food warehouses, silos, stables, etc. It can often be found in attics.

Compared to Brown Rat, Black is better at climbing and jumping, and can move very quickly on roof beams and rafters and from house to house using cables and wires. Black Rats do not dig tunnels in the earth, and they don't like to swim, which is why they are rarely found in open terrain; they will, however, build nests near houses high up in trees.

Black Rats are smaller and slimmer than Brown. They are 16–23 cm long, and the uniformly coloured tail is longer than that of Brown, 18–25 cm, and longer than its body. A Black Rat weighs 150–200 g.

Like that of Brown Rat, the coat of a Black Rat is variably dark grey to reddish brown, but it may also have a uniformly grey or almost black coat with a lighter underside. The Black Rat's snout is more pointed than Brown's, and its eyes and ears are larger, the ears being thin and fleshy grey in colour.

Black Rats are nocturnal, and like Brown Rats they live in large family groups.

The scat is shorter and thinner than that of Brown Rat, 1–1.2 cm long and 2–3 mm thick, often slightly bent and rounded at the ends. Black Rat's scat is found scattered in attics, while that of Brown Rat lies in piles near walls or in corners.

Both Black and Brown Rats will follow specific trails in attics. The trails can appear black, since the rats will urinate along them. Black Rat tracks resemble those of Brown but are slightly smaller. Drag marks from the tail will always show in dust.

Black Rats can spread dangerous diseases; luckily they are now rare in many areas. HW.

Brown Rat. Biopix.

Brown Rat

Rattus norvegicus

Brown Rats can be found wherever humans live, and many places nearby, including sewers, farms, dumps, and railroad facilities, as well as ports and along rivers and streams, near lakes, ponds, canals, and beaches, and in bird colonies. In autumn, rats living in more exposed areas look for a winter home. Brown Rats live in family groups that can become very large.

Brown Rats are about 21–29 cm long; a female weighs about 200 g, males are somewhat heavier at 250–300 g, and in some cases more than 500 g. The coat is greyish brown above and greyish white below. Individual Brown Rats may also have an almost black coat. The front legs are flesh pink, and there is a light spot on the chest.

The ears are large, pale, and covered with short hairs. The tail is 17–23 cm long

Brown Rat tracks in snow. TJ.

Brown Rats can have numerous litters each year. EAJ.

with short, stiff bristles that are light on the underside. The tail is slightly shorter than the body.

Young rats are a uniform grey and have a dark tail. They may resemble House Mice, but rats have a squatter body, a relatively larger head in comparison with the body, powerful hind feet, and a tail that is thick at its root. Black Rat is smaller and slimmer than Brown, has a more pointed snout, larger eyes, and larger, thinner, naked ears. The Black Rat's tail is a uniform colour and somewhat longer than its body. Brown Rats look a little like Northern Water Voles, but the latter has a short

A rats' nest by a drainpipe. PW.

tail, short ears, and a soft brown coat. The Muskrat is larger and has a relatively shorter tail.

Rats are mostly nocturnal; they run or walk, but can jump almost 1 m vertically and several metres horizontally. They often move no more than a whisker's length when running or walking next to a wall. They are good swimmers and climbers. Unlike water voles, they do not dive when disturbed.

The front footprints are 1.8 cm long and 2.5 cm wide, the hind footprint, 3–4.5 cm long and 2.5 cm wide. The rats' hind footprints are longer than those of Northern Water Vole, but significantly smaller than those of Muskrat.

The scat is 1–2 cm long and 5–6 mm thick, often slightly pointed at one or both ends. Scat is often left at latrine spots in corners or along walls.

Rats dig underground tunnels, often with multiple entrances. These tunnels are normally no more than 0.5 m underground, but they can be so close to one another that they undermine embankments, dykes, foundations, and sewage pipes. Nests and supply areas are located in the tunnels. The earth is loosened with the front feet and then swept out into conical heaps in front of the entrance with the hind legs. The holes are 6–8 cm in diameter and connected by visible trails above ground. In contrast, no removed earth can be seen in front of a Northern Water Vole's hole. Voles often feed on plants near their entrance holes; rats do not. Roots and stalks within the holes are normally chewed off by water voles, while rats usually squeeze by these without eating them.

Rat holes in sewage and drainage pipes are dug from below towards the surface, and no excavated earth will be visible. The quantity of earth shifted by rats is often so significant, you can see visible depressions in the surface from their activity. Rats can undermine tiles or concrete in the same way.

In the wild, rats follow specific trails that are marked with urine and scent secretions; they are 5–10 cm wide. These trails can be quite visible in attics and cellars in buildings, appearing as dark, grimy tracks as a result of urine and gland secretions from animals as they use the trails. Rat scat is usually clearly visible along these trails.

Rat nests, about 15 cm in diameter, are built from any kind of soft material, in the wild from grass and leaves, in man-made structures from straw, hay, paper, fabric, etc. In buildings, nests are often built under floors, in hollow walls, or between stacked goods.

Rats eat almost anything, but they prefer grain and seeds. At the shore they will eat snails, mussels, crabs, dead fish, and other carrion; in bird colonies they steal eggs and young, in the water they catch small fish, and small rodents may also become their prey. Rats will displace mice

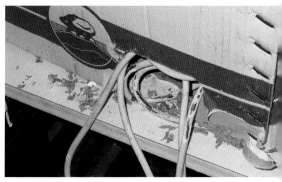

Rats in a trunk. Even the electric cords are gnawed. PW.

and voles. With their powerful teeth they can gnaw through anything that would need a knife to cut. The marks of both front teeth together are about 3 mm wide.

Rats gnaw one end of a grain kernel and what's left then consists of larger or smaller end pieces, but mice gnaw grain kernels from the side.

When rats gnaw at turnips, they begin from above and gnaw into the turnip; the tip then falls off and the turnip becomes an empty shell as it is eaten. Northern Water Voles gnaw at turnips from below.

Beware! One should never touch a dead rat or its scat since the urine contains bacteria that can cause leptospirosis. The disease, which can be deadly, causes flu-like symptoms, and the bacteria can attack the liver and kidneys.

Rats can gnaw through anything that would need a knife to cut. Biopix.

House Mouse
Mus musculus

House Mouse is a true mouse. It inhabits human settlements and can live and multiply in enclosed spaces, even under extreme conditions, for example, in cold-storage rooms with temperatures below freezing. It can survive for long periods without water.

House Mouse has two morphs—dark and light. The light morph is light grey to greyish brown on its back and light grey to white on its belly, and is common in eastern Europe. The dark morph is dark grey to greyish black on the back, and is especially widespread in western Europe.

In summer, the light morph is found near buildings and in gardens and parks, hedgerows, bushes, open woodland, and

areas with tall grass, only rarely in cultivated fields since these have insufficient insects, green plants, or weed seeds. In autumn the light morph moves inside. Dark-morph House Mice live mostly indoors year-round.

The eyes, ears, and tail are smaller than those of Wood Mouse. House Mouse is

The House Mouse has a distinctive smell. Biopix.

7.5–10 cm long, and the tail is 7–10 cm. It weighs 12–28 g. The tail is uniformly coloured, the same length as the body or a little shorter.

House Mouse prefers cereals and plant seeds but also eats plants and insects. Indoor mice will eat almost anything, for example, soap and candles. They will also create numerous food caches. Feeding areas are often dirtied with urine and scat.

House Mouse has four toes on the forefoot and five on the hind. The front print is about 1 cm long and 1.3 cm wide, the hind print up to 1.8 cm long and 1.8 cm wide. On soft terrain, in sand, dust, or sawdust, you can clearly see the tracks of the tail. House Mice follow clearly marked paths both inside and outside, and they travel them by walking rather than hopping or jumping, unlike Yellow-necked Mouse and Wood Mouse. The tracks are half the size of those of rats.

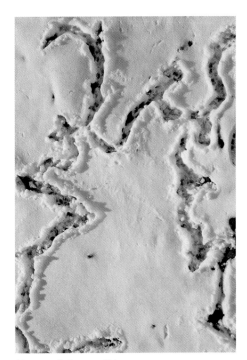

Mouse tracks in snow. PN.

Mice leave pungent-smelling scat and urine everywhere, scent-marking their presence for other mice. This is why food can attract bacteria; for example, *Salmonella* can be transmitted to humans and other animals in this way. The scat of Yellow-necked and Wood Mice does not smell.

House Mouse scat is about 6 mm long and 2–2.5 mm thick; rat scat can be up to 17 mm long and 4.6 mm thick.

House Mice are good climbers and swimmers; young mice can squeeze through cracks no wider than 7–8 mm, adult mice through gaps about 1 cm wide. They can chew through a great diversity of materials with their sharp teeth, and they leave holes in cupboards, floorboards, and insulation. Mouse holes are about 2 cm in diameter, rat holes about 5–7 cm. The gnaw marks left by the front teeth of a House Mouse are less than 2 mm wide, those left by rats, about 3 mm.

Where building materials are soft, House Mice can create tunnel systems 2–3 cm in diameter where they make nests and store food. Conical nests of dried grass, about 10 cm in diameter, are built outdoors; indoor nests are constructed with all kinds of materials, including paper,

A House Mouse is sexually mature after two months, and a litter often comprises 10–12 young.

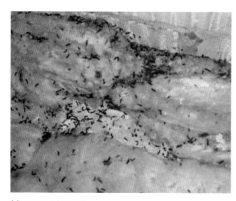

Mouse scat in meat.

pieces of fabric, insulation, straw, feathers, and wood shavings.

House Mice eat grain kernels from the side, holding them with their front feet. You can see tooth marks on gnawed kernels. Rats start gnawing a kernel from the end.

Beware! Mice and rats can transmit *Salmonella* to humans. If you touch mice or rats when removing them from traps, or touch old, used traps without wearing gloves, you must wash your hands thoroughly afterwards. A salmonella infection can be very unpleasant, even deadly.

Mice can cause considerable damage by chewing fabric. LS.

Yellow-necked Mouse can be confused with a young rat, but its back and belly are clearly different colours. AK.

Yellow-necked Mouse

Apodemus flavicollis

Yellow-necked Mouse is a true mouse. It has an orange-brown back clearly distinct from its chalk-white belly. Distinguishing marks are its size and the yellowish brown patch on its lower throat that broadens to a wider patch between the front legs.

Yellow-necked Mouse is almost twice the size of a House Mouse. It is frequently confused with Wood Mouse, which is greyish brown above and greyish white below. Wood Mouse has a restricted area of colour on the lower throat instead of the yellowish brown patch, and its snout is not as long.

Yellow-necked Mouse has large eyes and ears, and a tail longer than its body. The nose is comparatively long, the body about 8–13 cm in length, and the tail 9.5–13.5 cm, and the mouse weighs 12–55 g.

Yellow-necked Mice live in woods, bushes, parks, and gardens, but can also be found in fields with turnips, rape, and peas, although never in open fields. This is the only mouse species that inhabits beech woods and extensive fir plantations, and it can jump and climb better than any other true mouse. You can even find Yellow-necked Mice in the treetops, and they occasionally sleep in nest boxes or squirrel or birds' nests. If they feel threatened they will try to climb, while Wood Mice will hide in grass or moss.

195

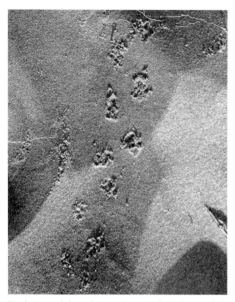

Tracks in sand show the jumping gait of a Yellow-necked Mouse.

In deep loose snow you will see tail tracks. Biopix.

Food remains at the entrance to a Yellow-necked Mouse's burrow. NWK.

During winter they like to move into buildings. Yellow-necked and House Mice and rats are the only rodents that inhabit buildings for prolonged periods of time, and they are found mostly in attics. They have replaced House Mouse in many areas as the most common species found in human habitations.

Yellow-necked Mice are mostly nocturnal, but in winter they are occasionally visible during the day, for example, when they take something from a bird feeder.

You don't always see tail marks in the snow, since the mouse stretches out the tail when jumping. The length of the jump is normally about 20 cm, but it can be more than 1 m. The tracks are similar to those of a squirrel but smaller. The footprints are set close together, but those of the large hind feet are in front and further out.

Yellow-necked Mice have five toes on both front and hind feet, but the innermost toe on the forefoot sits high, so it is not always visible in the print, in which case the track of the forefoot will show the imprint of only four toes. The prints are 16 mm long and 18 mm wide. The hind footprint also shows five toes, the inner being very long, while the outer and especially the big toe are very short; the prints are 22–24 mm long, and 19 mm wide.

Yellow-necked Mice dig a tunnel system up to 1 m deep, containing one or more nests and food caches. The nesting areas are large and built with straw and dry leaves. When a Yellow-necked Mouse builds a new hole, the earth is expelled in a fan-shaped pattern and forms large mounds in front of the hole.

Yellow-necked Mice prefer large seeds such as acorns, hazelnuts, and beechnuts, cereals, and the stones of fruit, rose hips, etc., which they collect and cache on the forest floor, under brushwood, under fallen trees, in hollows, in attics, in nest boxes, etc. They can also build nests of dry leaves in winter at these locations, and these nests are also cushioned with moss and grass.

Cones gnawed by mice are identifiable because the scales are gnawed closer to the cone's axis, and the teeth marks of mice are more regular than you see when squirrels have been feeding; moreover, the frayed tip at the cone's base is missing, and mice leave fewer scales on the tip than squirrels do. In

thick conifer forest, you can assume that mouse-damaged cones have been eaten by Yellow-necked Mice, because other mouse species are rare in this habitat.

Yellow-necked Mouse does not usually climb trees for cones, but makes do with those that have fallen or were lost by squirrels. You find cones with signs of mouse feeding in concealed places, where the mouse has eaten in hiding. At these sites it is difficult to determine whether a Yellow-necked Mouse, a Wood Mouse, or a Bank Vole has dined on the cones.

On a hazelnut, the tooth marks of a Yellow-necked Mouse can be identified from the small ring shapes made by the mouse's upper teeth. Once the mouse has bitten a hole, it places the nut on the

Yellow-necked Mice have a yellow-brown band between the front legs. LG.

Yellow-necked Mouse can be identified from its yellow-brown lower throat and neck, large ears, and long tail. Biopix.

ground and gnaws at the edge furthest from its body from the inside out, using the lower teeth. The same approach is also used by Wood Mice, Northern Water Voles, and Common Dormice, and this type of tooth mark can also be found on the stones of cherries, plums, and sloes. Yellow-necked Mice open beechnuts by gnawing an irregular hole on one side of the nut at the widest end, then extracting the contents. You find clear tooth marks on the shells, and the shells are piled in heaps at feeding sites.

Unlike squirrels, Yellow-necked Mice have insufficient strength to pry walnut shells apart, so they gnaw through the shells, leaving numerous regular and small tooth marks behind.

Grain kernels are also gnawed from the side, in exactly the same way as humans eat corn on the cob.

The scat of Yellow-necked Mouse has no smell, and it is shorter and thicker than that of House Mouse, about 5 mm long and 2.5 mm thick.

Wood Mouse

Apodemus sylvaticus

The Wood Mouse is another true mouse and resembles a small Yellow-necked Mouse. It has large eyes and ears, is greyish brown above, and greyish white below. It can be distinguished from Yellow-necked Mouse by its somewhat shorter tail. It has an elongated yellowish brown spot between its front legs; Yellow-necked Mouse has a continuous yellowish brown band.

Wood Mice are 7.5–10.5 cm long and weigh 8–28 g; the tail is 7–9.5 cm long, so a little shorter than the body.

In spite of its name, in northern Europe you usually find Wood Mice in open landscapes, cultivated fields, hedgerows, meadows, fallow fields, as well as areas with heath or dunes. They also like young plantations, but only rarely woodland, from which they are largely displaced by Yellow-necked Mice. In other parts of Europe they will inhabit woodland.

In autumn, many Wood Mice move from open landscapes to the edge of woodland, stone walls, or into uncultivated areas with small trees and tall grass. In northern Europe, unlike further south, they can frequently be found in attics and other areas in houses.

Wood Mice are seldom active during the day, unlike Common Voles and Bank Voles. They can often evade predators thanks to their speed, while voles will hide in vegetation and remain in their tunnels at the sign of danger.

The tracks of a Wood Mouse resemble those of Yellow-necked Mouse, but the hind foot is shorter, about 21–22 mm. Wood Mice move in jumps, and the tracks of the two species can be separated only by careful observations. Like a Yellow-necked Mouse, a Wood Mouse digs really deep underground tunnels; the nests are often so deep they are not destroyed when fields are ploughed. When holes are dug from the outside you

The Wood Mouse is smaller than Yellow-necked Mouse and has a shorter tail and a yellowish brown spot between the front legs. LG.

Wood Mice love beechnuts. LG.

will see expelled mounds of earth. The deep tunnels are used mainly in winter; in summer the mice dig tunnels closer to the surface and less intricate in design.

Wood Mice feed mostly on grain kernels and weeds, nuts and fruit, as well as green plants and numerous insects, worms, and snails, especially in areas with dunes and heath. You can find the remains of a Wood Mouse's meal in sheltered spots under clumps of grass, branches, stones, or tree trunks, but also just in front of the mouse's

Wood Mice readily eat grain and weed seeds. Biopix.

hole. The Wood Mouse handles cones and nuts in the same way as Yellow-necked Mouse; the scat is also similar.

Striped Field Mouse
Apodemus agrarius

The Striped Field Mouse gets its name from the pronounced black stripe extending down its back from its ears to its tail. Northern Birch Mouse also has a black stripe on its back but this extends all the way to its eyes. The tail of the Striped Field Mouse is shorter than its body, whereas the tail of a Northern Birch Mouse is longer than its body.

In summer, Striped Field Mice are a rich brown; in winter, somewhat lighter. They are 9.5–12 cm long; the tail is 6.5–9 cm long, about two-thirds the length of the body. They weigh 16–25 g. In summer they may become a shiny reddish brown above, in the winter a duller greyish brown, and underneath they are a greyish white all year-round.

They live mostly in open pasture, wet meadows, fallow fields, field edges, the edges of woodland, and in hedgerows; in eastern Europe they can often be found in parks and gardens. In winter they take refuge in houses and barns and you can then find them in turnip or potato 'clamps' (piles of vegetables covered with earth).

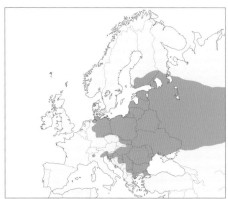

Striped Field Mice dig underground tunnel systems with nests and food caches, but these tunnels are not far below the surface. The mice are active day and night. They feed mainly on seeds and fruit but may also eat insects, worms, and snails or gnaw at carrion.

Striped Field Mice will walk or run; they don't jump or climb as well as Yellow-necked or Wood Mice. The tracks are similar to those of Wood and Yellow-necked Mice, but the hind footprints are somewhat smaller, 16–18 mm.

They gnaw on nuts in the same fashion as Bank Voles. The nut is held with the point facing away from the mouse and under the mouse's chest. After gnawing a hole in the nut, the mouse puts its snout in the hole and, using its lower teeth, eats

Striped Field Mice relish hazelnuts. LG.

Striped Field Mice can be identified by the black stripe on the back. LG.

from the outside in, on the closest edge. This is how a sharp edge is formed in the nutshell but with no tooth marks on the outside.

A Striped Field Mouse's cache of nuts.

Harvest Mouse

Micromys minutus

The Harvest Mouse is 5.5–7.5 cm long, the tail is 5–7 cm long, and the animal weighs 5–9 g. In summer it is yellowish brown above, white underneath. In winter it is a dark orange-brown and has a greyish belly; at the root of the tail and on the back of the legs it is ochre-coloured. The eyes and ears are relatively small.

Harvest Mice usually live in cereal fields and areas with tall grass, as well as reed belts, the borders of fields, woodland edges, and hedgerows. Harvest Mice usually stay in vegetation, using the long tail to hold onto twigs and branches. The mice feed on plant seeds, soft plant tissue, and a variety of insects. Harvest Mice don't hibernate.

The front footprint is 0.8 cm long and 6.5–7 mm wide, the hind footprint is 1.3 cm long and 1 cm wide. The prints resemble those of a shrew, but a shrew's footprints are usually found between the stalks of plants on which they have been feeding.

Harvest Mice are good climbers and can often be found high up in the vegetation. LG.

Harvest Mice build nests from fresh plants which then wilt. LG.

Harvest Mice are often found in cereal fields. Biopix.

The scat is 2 mm long and usually found around the nest.

In summer a breeding nest is built between tall grass stalks, normally situated about a half metre from the ground, but it can be found up to a height of 1 m. The nest might also be found in thick underbrush or on the lower branches of young conifers. The nest is spherical with a diameter of 8–10 cm, and is woven with grass stalks split lengthwise, and cushioned with soft plant tissue. The twigs and leaves of living plants are woven into the structure for support, so the nest is well camouflaged the entire summer. The nest normally has no obvious entrance, the female forcing herself inside prior to giving birth. In most cases the young destroy the nest and a new one is built fresh for each litter.

Harvest Mice build additional small nests nearby where they can hide during the day. These may have two entrances, one opposite the other. When the plants wither in the fall, the nests appear as small balls of hay and resemble the nests of wrens, but the latter will always contain down. During mild winters the nest may be built between plants, but normally it would be found in hollows in the earth, under clumps of grass, stones, or tree roots. Harvest Mice can also live in piles of hay or straw, or in barns or sheds, where they store food supplies of grain and wild plant seeds.

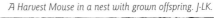

A Harvest Mouse in a nest with grown offspring. J-LK.

Northern Birch Mouse
Sicista betulina

Northern Birch Mouse is greyish brown with a narrow black stripe along its back, extending from the tail over the head to the eyes; the tail is also significantly longer than the body—up to 1.5 times as long. The Striped Field Mouse has a similar black stripe on its back, but this extends only to the forehead; moreover, the tail of the Striped Field Mouse is shorter than its body, and, overall, Striped Field is almost twice the size of Northern Birch.

Northern Birch Mouse is as large as a Harvest Mouse, 5–7 cm long; the tail is 8–11 cm, so 1.5 times the body length. Northern Birch Mice weigh 6.5–13 g, and the fur is greyish brown to yellowish brown above, and greyish white below.

Northern Birch Mice are nocturnal. They can be found in many places—near embankments and dykes and in hilly landscapes or river valleys, thick hedgerows, clumps of willow, birch woodland, open woodland with thick underbrush, moorland with bushes, heathland, and meadows, especially in damper areas and near water.

Northern Birch Mice hibernate in winter, when they look for protected and dry areas, for instance, woodland, bushes, embankments, or dykes. You can find winter nests in old tree stumps or small holes in the ground dug by the mice themselves. You very rarely find Northern Birch Mice in buildings.

These mice do not build underground tunnels; instead they use natural hollows, the tunnel systems of other small rodents, hollows in trees, and holes below boulders or in overturned trees.

They feed mostly on plants, fresh shoots, buds, and berries, but also eat insects, earthworms, and snails, which they often find by removing the bark from old rotting trees. They are good climbers and may be seen high up in bushes and trees. The five toes of the hind foot can be used by the mice like a hand, and they also use the long, supple tail for support. Their tracks resemble those of Harvest Mice.

The Northern Birch Mouse resembles a Striped Field Mouse, but it is significantly smaller, the black stripe on the back reaches as far as the eyes, and the tail is significantly longer than the body. BL.

Common Dormouse

Muscardinus avellanarius

Common Dormouse, also known as Hazel Dormouse, is the same size as a House Mouse. It has a short snout and long whiskers, large, dark eyes, and hairy ears. Its body is compact, 6 cm long, and it weighs 15–40 g, a little more in autumn. It is reddish or orange-brown above and yellowish brown below with a white throat and chest. The tail is 5.5–7.5 cm long. The long hair gives the animals something of a bushy appearance.

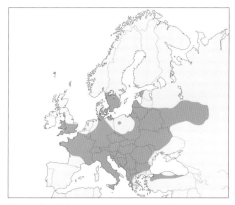

Common Dormouse lives in deciduous and mixed woodland with thick and varied underbrush but may also be found in open landscapes with bushes, or in gardens and parks and also occasionally in buildings. The dormice prefer locations where they can avoid being on the ground.

Common Dormice are nocturnal; during the day they lie curled up in their nests. If disturbed, they climb up plants, where they stay for a while and look around, like squirrels. Common Dormouse is very active and a good climber. It has long, flexible toes and the hind feet can be turned at right angles to the body.

In spring Common Dormouse feeds on leaf buds, young shoots, and blossoms; in summer it consumes a variety of insects, and in autumn, berries, beechnuts, and nuts. Common Dormice hibernate. They move in jumps, and the tracks, if seen, strongly suggest a tiny squirrel.

You almost never see the tracks of Common Dormice, but you can find their nests in thick underbrush, in trees, nest boxes, or hollow trees, normally 1–4 m above the ground.

If a Common Dormouse is disturbed, it sits very still and watches alertly. LG.

Common Dormice have large pads on their feet, powerful claws, and a brown, hairy tail.

The nest is spherical, about 10–15 cm in diameter and very similar to the nests of wrens and Long-tailed Tits. It is built of dried grass, leaves, lichens, moss and bark, all carefully woven together. Now and again a bird's nest is used as the foundation. On the inside it is cushioned with plant fibres, etc. The lateral entrance hole is normally sealed. There are often many nests close together. In winter the summer nests of wrens may be used by dormice.

Winter nests are built on the ground under tree stumps, between roots or under stones, and they can also be found in hollow trees or nest boxes. They normally contain plenty of moss and are often built with the stems of rosebay willowherb.

Common Dormouse gnaws very even holes in hazelnuts. Like Wood Mouse, it eats the nut from the inside out, but the tooth marks are so weak that the gnawed edge seems almost smooth. Nuts are consumed in bushes or in trees, and the discarded shells are scattered below.

Winter nest of a Common Dormouse in a blackberry hedge. PB.

Summer nest of a Common Dormouse.

Garden Dormouse

Eliomys quercinus

Garden Dormouse is easy to identify. It is 10–17 cm long and weighs 50–100 g, somewhat more in autumn. It is greyish brown above, white below. The ears are very large, and it has an extensive dark spot around the eyes and under the ears.

The tail is 9–15 cm long and covered with short, thick hairs, which end in a tuft at the tip. The front upperparts of the body are greyish brown, black further down its back. The tail is white underneath, with a white tip.

Garden Dormice are usually found in conifer forest and orchards as well as in gardens and parks with rocks, stone walls, hollow trees, sheds, etc. They are active at night and are good climbers but spend much time on the ground. Garden Dormice hibernate.

Garden Dormice feed on small animals such as insects, snails, and other invertebrates as well as frogs, lizards, young birds, and small mammals; also green shoots, berries, and fruit. They feed on apples still hanging on the tree, and the tooth marks are then clearly visible.

The Garden Dormouse is a good climber. You find its nests in hollow trees, nest boxes or stone walls, rarely on the ground. DN.

The tracks of a Garden Dormouse resemble those of other mice, but are larger. They are similar to a squirrel's but narrower. The forefoot has five toes, but the innermost is significantly smaller and cannot be seen in the print. The front footprints are about 3 cm long and the same width. The hind foot also has five toes; the footprints are about 4 cm long and 3 cm wide. On soft terrain you can often see tracks left by the tail.

The nest of a Garden Dormouse is easy to identify; it is spherical with a lateral entrance and made of grass and moss. Inside it is cushioned with moss, hair, and down. The nest is built in an old squirrel or birds' nest, in a hollow tree or nest box, between rocks, or in brushwood, a wood pile, or a hole in the ground. Winter nests are also found in buildings, cellars, and other storage areas, and in walls.

Nest of a Garden Dormouse in a nest box.

The nest is built of grass and cushioned with moss and may be camouflaged with leaves, as one can see above.

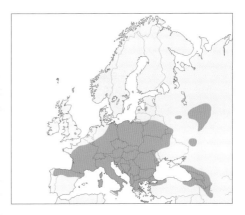

Edible Dormouse. IA.

Edible Dormouse

Glis glis

Edible Dormouse gets its name from the days of ancient Rome, when they were fattened in special earthenware containers before being eaten. Edible Dormouse is a relatively large animal, about 12–20 cm long and weighing 70– 250 g. It is silver grey above and white or slightly yellow below. The area around the large and prominent eyes is dark. The tail is 11–16 cm long and very bushy. Except for the colour, this dormouse resembles a squirrel.

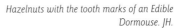

Hazelnuts with the tooth marks of an Edible Dormouse. JH.

As with other dormice, Edible Dormouse is largely nocturnal but may be seen at dusk. Edible Dormouse is very active and a good climber. It can be found in deciduous woodland, where it stays mainly in bushes or lower trees, but it can also occur in gardens, parks, and orchards. In autumn you occasionally come across it in a building, especially attics and sheds. Edible Dormice can jump long distances, climb up smooth walls, and are very social animals.

They are herbivores, and prefer fruit and nuts but also consume small animals, birds' eggs, and small birds. They may also feed on bark, especially that of fruit trees. Nuts are not cracked; instead the dormice will chew irregular holes in them to extract the contents.

In summer Edible Dormice build nests of dried leaves and grass and position them high up in trees. In autumn they dig underground tunnels, in which they build a nest

An Edible Dormouse in its nest in a hollow tree. CZ.

for hibernation. Their tracks are similar to a squirrel's but somewhat smaller.

Edible Dormice may also use attics for hibernation.

The tail of an Edible Dormouse is large and bushy, very similar to a squirrel's.

The Northern Red-backed Vole has large eyes and is not particularly shy. SS.

Voles have short legs and very short tails. They are built more compactly than true mice and move more slowly and ploddingly; most of the species walk or run but rarely jump. Their footprints resemble those of martens. The footprints are found next to one another, the hind prints overlapping the front. Occasionally you might see the track of the short tail.

Their scat is usually smooth and round.

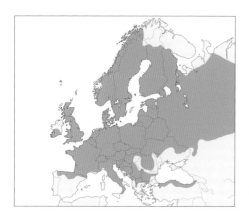

Bank Vole

Clethrionomys glareolus

The Bank Vole has a greyish brown back; the undersides are greyish white. It is heavy for a vole and weighs 11–30 g and is 8–12.5 cm long; the tail measures 3.5–7 cm, so usually about half the body length. Despite its weight it is relatively slim, has large eyes and a tail that is longer than that of Common Vole, sometimes up to two-thirds of the body length.

Bank Voles prefer deciduous or mixed woodland with thick ground cover and piles of brushwood, but they also live in conifer forest with clearings and damper areas. They can also be found in underbrush and hedgerows as well as in swamps with reeds and alders; they can also occur in older gardens with brushwood and plenty of trees and bushes. They avoid open fields.

Bank Voles are active day and night and not particularly shy. They dig fairly shallow

The entrance to a Bank Vole's nest.

Cherry stones with the tooth marks of Bank Vole. LG.

tunnels, but can also be found under cliffs and boulders, clumps of grass, fallen tree trunks, and under tree roots. Their spherical nests are 10–15 cm in diameter and made of grass, leaves, moss, bark fibres, etc. These nests are used not only during breeding season, but also as feeding sites and for food storage. In autumn, Bank Voles may look for buildings to winter in.

The front footprints are about 11 mm wide and 13 mm long, the hind prints 15 mm wide and 17 mm long. The Bank Vole usually moves in short jumps; consequently the hind prints are imprinted on top of the front.

The track ends in a hole in the ground, in snow, or in a tree or bush. Bank Voles feed on green plants, berries, buds, shoots, bark, and seeds. In northern Scandinavia they eat mushrooms and lichens, mostly boletes and beard lichens. You can see the marks of their front teeth on a mushroom cap, and these are about 1.5–2 mm wide. Bank Voles feed on cones in the same fashion as Yellow-necked and Wood Mice, and on nuts and cherry and plum stones in the same way as Striped Field Mice (*cf.* p. 201).

Bank Voles like rose hips and apples, consuming the fruit's flesh but not the seeds.

In autumn they gather supplies of grain, nuts, acorns, beechnuts, cherry stones, etc. and place these in holes in the ground, hollow trees, and nest boxes. When a Bank Vole fails to find its stored food, or is killed before it can use them, the seeds may sprout. Hoards of beechnuts that sprout in this fashion have come to be known as 'mouse-beeches', in other words, beeches that grow tightly bunched.

Bank Voles are agile climbers and chew on the bark of young conifers, deciduous trees, and bushes, and may completely chew off elderberry branches. This will happen especially in years with large vole populations.

Bank Voles do not feed on the lower part of a trunk, but higher up in the tree. They start at a branch fork and go along the branch removing bark. Under the gnawed trees you will find small pieces of gnawed-off bark: these are the external layers of thick bark, removed so the voles can get to the inner, more succulent part of the tree. The bark may show groove-shaped tooth marks 1.5–2 mm wide.

Field Vole

Microtus agrestis

Field Voles look very similar to Common Voles. Like other voles, Field Vole has a short tail, short legs, a rounded head, and ears that are almost entirely covered by fur. This vole is about 9.5–13.5 cm long, the tail 3–4.5 cm, and it weighs 19–52 g. It is dark brown above, the belly is white, and the tail also has a light underside.

Field Voles live in open areas with tall, thick grass. When Field Vole inhabits the same areas as Common, Field will prefer damper areas, while Common favours drier areas with shorter grass. Field Vole feeds almost exclusively on grass; since this diet is not very nutritious, it must forage both day and night. It also eats plants such as clover and dandelion and bark in winter. It rarely moves into buildings in autumn.

The tracks of Field Voles are not easily separated from those of other voles and mice. It usually walks; because of its short legs, it cannot jump or climb very

well. Tracks of the feet and tail leave a rut in soft snow; the hind footprint is about 18 mm long.

Field Voles use long, partially covered trails leading from one hole to another in a tunnel system just below thick grass, where you can find short stems of gnawed-off grass. The nest is 15 cm in diameter and woven from grass; it can be under ground, or under a clump of grass or a stone above ground.

In winter, voles dig tunnels under the snow, where they feed on plants. Nests

The Field Vole has a short tail and small ears covered by long hairs. LG.

Field Voles prefer tall vegetation, including cereal fields. LG.

brownish in summer. You can find scat in the tunnel systems, often collected in mounds.

Field Voles chew the stems of common rush or raspberries, leaving small white fragments 10–15 cm long at their feeding sites. They also bite off dandelion blossoms to reach unripe seeds; the silky white pappi are left behind in a heap.

Field Voles may chew the bark off young trees from the roots up to a height of about 15 cm, and this will often kill the tree.

might also be built here. Once the snow melts, you can see parts of the tunnel system with its earth walls and chewed-off grass stems littering the tunnels.

The scat is the size of rice grains, 6–7 mm long and 2–3 mm thick. In winter the scat is yellowish green; darker green or

The voles prefer small deciduous trees, but will also feed on conifers if there is nothing else. In gardens and orchards, Field Voles can cause significant damage to the roots of old trees. You will see entrances to the tunnel system near damaged trees.

After snow has melted, Field Vole tunnels are clearly visible. NO.

When snow cover is thin, Field Voles dig visible tunnels in the snow. LG.

Common Vole
Microtus arvalis

Common Vole resembles Field Vole so closely that it is almost impossible to tell them apart, but Common is somewhat smaller overall and a little more yellowish brown on the upperparts. Common Vole is about 9.5–12 cm long and the tail measures 3–4.5 cm; it weighs 14–46 g.

Common Vole eats mainly grass and can be found in drier areas than those favoured by Field Vole. It lives where the plant cover is not too tall and thick and can therefore be found in grassy fields, gardens, and parks. Common Vole digs larger underground tunnel systems than those constructed by a Field Vole. The entrance holes are about 3 cm in diameter and connected by trails in the grass that can be several metres long; Common Voles rarely move away from these trails. Common Voles are not very active during the day since they cannot hide easily in the habitat they favour. They do not feed on bark as much as Field Voles like to.

The tracks are identical to those of Field Vole, but Common Voles do not move into buildings in autumn.

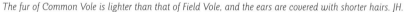

The fur of Common Vole is lighter than that of Field Vole, and the ears are covered with shorter hairs. JH.

Norway Lemming
Lemmus lemmus

The Norway Lemming is also known simply as Lemming; it is easily identified by the black on top of its head and upper back, as well as by the two orange spots on its ears. The lower back is reddish brown with black stripes in the middle and on both sides of the body; the undersides are grey.

It is 7–15.5 cm long and the tail is 1.5–2 cm long; it weighs up to 110 g.

Norway Lemmings inhabit rocky heathland areas above the treeline, and in summer are found near water and in moorland. They dig large tunnel systems in the moss cover, smaller ones in the ground. In winter they prefer drier areas with rocks and moss, often on rocky slopes on which the snow can gather in an insulating layer, under which they build long tunnels that become visible when the snow melts.

Norway Lemmings feed mainly on moss, lichens, sedges, cotton grass, and other grasses; they also eat berries, blossoms, and the leaves of small trees and bushes, and

sometimes mushrooms. They are active all day. The tracks resemble those of Common and Northern Red-backed Voles, but the latter species do not normally occur in high mountain areas.

Norway Lemmings are known for their population fluctuations; some years they can be so numerous, they wander into areas where they are normally absent. These wanderings are probably caused by a scarcity of food.

Norway Lemmings normally do not jump but walk; on firm terrain they rarely follow a straight line, but move in a serpentine pattern. Their tracks can be seen especially well in the snow and will always end or begin at a hole. The footprints are splayed and normally a tail print is not visible.

The scat resembles that of other voles; it may occasionally be found in great quantities at feeding or nest sites.

Norway Lemmings can be identified by their black heads with light spots above the ears. ME.

Norway Lemmings love succulent plants. SS.

Nest of a Norway Lemming after the snow has melted. Biopix.

The scat is about 7 mm long and 3 mm thick, yellowish green or brown.

Norway Lemmings build nests between stones and rocks, and these may lie relatively exposed between plants. After snow has melted in spring, nests that were built in the winter are visible; they are 20–25 cm in diameter and consist of grass and moss arranged in clearly visible clumps in mountain moorland.

The scat is often in heaps in front of the entrance to the burrow. AK

Wood Lemming
Myopus schisticolor

Wood Lemmings are greyish black on the upperparts with a rust-brown area on the back; the undersides are somewhat lighter. Wood Lemmings are 6.5–11.5 cm long, the tail measures 0.9–1.8 cm, and the animal weighs 10–45 g.

Wood Lemmings are found in moorland and damp conifer forest (particularly spruce) with thick moss. They feed mainly on moss and lichens, but also eat grass, reeds, and horsetails. Their tracks resemble those of other voles, especially those of Norway Lemming. The scat can be light green when really fresh, about 8 mm long; older scat is yellowish brown. Wood Lemmings are nocturnal and active year-round.

Wood Lemmings also experience population booms and at these times will wander far and wide. Their tunnels in the moss may be clearly visible. Wood Lemmings eat the top layer of moss, and these grazed areas then stand out as lighter spots in the landscape.

Wood Lemming is smaller than Norway Lemming and has no black patches in its dark brown to slate grey fur. KBA.

Grey-sided Voles are endemic to Scandinavian mountain regions. SS.

Grey-sided Vole

Clethrionomys rufocanus

Grey-sided Vole is a little larger than Bank Vole, but has a shorter tail and ears and stronger reddish colouration on the back. The sides of the body and the cheeks are grey, the belly light grey. It is 9–13.5 cm long, and the tail measures 2.5–4 cm, so about one-quarter of the body length. This vole weighs 20–50 g. Grey-sided is somewhat slow and clumsy, but compared with Common can climb relatively well.

Grey-sided Voles occur in the higher mountain regions of Scandinavia, especially in conifer and birch forest. They are active throughout the day. They build a spherical nest of grass, branches, moss, and strips of bark; nests are about 15 cm in diameter and can be found under stones, trees, and roots and between rocks. Grey-sided Voles do not excavate underground tunnels, but they will move beneath snow.

Their footprints resemble those of Bank Vole but are somewhat larger; the hind footprint is 18–19 mm long. As is the case with Bank Vole, they store food, but Grey-sided does not gnaw on bark as frequently.

Grey-sided Voles live mostly on green plants, berries, blueberry plants, moss, and grass.

Root Vole

Microtus oeconomus

Root Vole is the largest vole in Scandinavia. It resembles Common Vole, but is a little larger, darker on the upper side, and has a distinct bicoloured tail that is dark above and light below. Root Vole is about 10–15 cm long, with a 3–6 cm tail, and weighs 20–75 g.

It lives in swampy or very damp areas with dense vegetation, as well as in meadows and near ponds up to coastal regions, but may also live in wet woodland, moorland, and near lakes and flowing water, but it looks for drier regions in autumn. It can live in barns and sheds as well. Root Vole swims and dives well and is active throughout the day.

Root Vole moves along trails in the grass and digs extensive underground tunnels. Its tracks resemble those of other voles, but when digging, it can eject so much earth

from the tunnels that the piles resemble molehills. The nest is spherical and built either in an underground tunnel or above ground, under stones and rocks, tree roots, fallen trees, or thick clumps of grass.

Root Voles feed on green plants, grass, cotton grass, reeds, and horsetail; in winter, they feed on roots below ground. They also feed on bark.

The male Root Vole is significantly larger than the female. JH.

Common Mole

Talpa europaea

The Common Mole eats mostly earthworms and a variety of insects. It has a cylindrical body, without a visible neck, and is optimised for life below ground. It is 12–17 cm long with a 2.1–3.2 cm tail; the female weighs 60–90 g, the male 90–115 g. Common Moles have a black, velvety soft, bear-like coat that grows at right angles to the body. This is why they can move just as well both backwards and forward in their tunnels.

The mole has long feeler hairs on its pale red snout and the tip of its tail, as well as spread over the rest of its coat. As the mole travels through its tunnels, it keeps its tail up as a kind of antenna. It has a small pointed snout and very small eyes completely covered by fur; the ears are not visible.

You find Common Moles in fields and meadows, but also in gardens and deciduous woodland; they completely avoid sandy soil. The largest part of their diet comprises earthworms, but they also eat insects, insect larvae, and other invertebrates they encounter in their tunnels. Each individual lives in its own network of tunnels; however, these may be connected to other moles' tunnels.

Males and females are together only during the mating season. The tunnels can be used by other animals like voles or shrews. Above ground, you occasionally find a dead mole that was killed during a nightly outing. Many predators kill moles but do not consume them—perhaps they do not taste good.

A Common Mole's system of branching tunnels encompasses different levels and can stretch for 100–200 m. The deepest sections can lie 1 m underground, and these are used particularly during winter, when the Common Mole's prey withdraws more deeply

Molehills often lie in a row. Left. JJ; right. LG.

Moles shove the earth to the surface with their front feet. PB.

Moles are practically blind. The front legs are powerful digging devices with thick claws. LG.

into the earth. The tunnels are slightly oval, 4 cm high and about 5 cm wide.

Excess earth is heaped into hills that are found in two rough sizes. The smaller ones are made from excess earth from the tunnel system; the larger ones, fortresses, are sometimes built over an underground nest. The hills will often lie in a row, so you can follow the sequence of tunnels underground.

Common Moles also dig tunnels directly under the surface, which one can see as ridges 4–5 cm high. During this latter process no molehills are created.

Occasionally the mole leaves its underground tunnel system at night to find a new place to live, to look for prey on the surface, or to search for nesting materials or drinking water. When the mole leaves its tunnel, it always does so through a molehill

and never through a hole in the side like a vole. It leaves the hole open and closes it only after returning. If a hole hasn't been closed by daybreak, the mole is either dead or has found new living quarters.

The Common Mole's front feet are turned at an almost 180-degree angle to the body; they are very powerful and perfectly designed for digging. The front foot is enlarged and has an additional bone, giving the impression that the animal has six toes. When the mole moves above ground, it supports itself on the edges of its front feet, and this is why you see the prints of only the tips of the five powerful claws and the extra bone. The footprints lie in the direction of motion, slightly arched and one behind the other.

The hind foot has five toes, each with a claw; the footprint is about 1.5 cm long and 1 cm wide.

Tunnels running close to the surface.

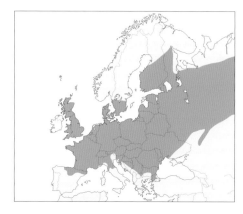

Western Hedgehog

Erinaceus europaeus

You cannot mistake a hedgehog—the upperparts are covered with 5,000–7,000 quills about 2–3 cm long and 2 mm thick. On its underside, Western Hedgehog has stiff brown hairs. If the animal feels threatened, it can tightly curl itself into a round ball, in this way protecting the whole body with the quills.

Western Hedgehog is 20–30 cm long, with a 3 cm tail, and weighs about 0.8–1.5 kg; it is heaviest in autumn, shortly before hibernation. Males are somewhat larger than females.

Western Hedgehogs are active from dusk until dawn. They make a lot of noise, snuffle all the time while searching for food, and eat noisily. They feed mainly on earthworms, earwigs, insect larvae, millipedes, and snails, but they also consume

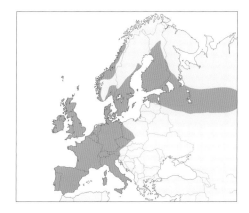

other small animals. They also gladly feed on carrion, and in summer and autumn eat fruit and berries.

Western Hedgehogs prefer living near human habitation, in gardens and parks, but can also be found in hedgerows, at woodland edges, or in clearings. They are

Western Hedgehogs are active between dusk and dawn. LG.

not normally found in open cultivated areas or extensive woodland.

Western Hedgehogs have five toes on all feet, but the inner toe leaves a very weak imprint, sometimes suggesting a four-toed animal. The footprints of front and hind feet are almost identical, about 2.5–4.5 cm long and 2.5–2.8 cm wide. The front footprint is wider than the hind and turned inward; the hind print is somewhat longer than the front and turned outwards. The stride is 15–25 cm and strongly splayed, and since Western Hedgehog has short legs, you often see drag marks from the belly.

The scat is large, firm, and strong-smelling. It can be found anywhere the animal is active. Scat is 0.8–1 cm thick, 3–5 cm long, and pointed at one end. It is shiny black and contains the remains of insects; at the end of summer and in autumn, it also contains berries. Occasionally you might also find hair, feathers, and small pieces of bone in the scat. If the hedgehog has eaten only mice or birds, the scat is dull-coloured, twisted, and very thin.

Hedgehog scat is black and hard. LG.

You will often find small holes in the earth, along with scat, in a field; these are the result of the hedgehog drilling with its snout in search of insect larvae. The holes are smaller than those left by badgers. Though they have powerful claws, hedgehogs do not generally dig in the ground.

Western Hedgehogs will occasionally eat eggs and the young of colonial ground-breeding birds, and they may consume large quantities of both. They bite irregular holes in the side of an egg and lick out the contents; chicken eggs

Western Hedgehog tracks in mud. KG.

Hedgehogs rarely run. LG.

are, however, too large for hedgehogs to handle.

Western Hedgehogs normally build underground nests. In spring the female builds a nest in a quiet place under thick bushes, in a hedge, in a hollow, in a shed, etc. The ground is cushioned with grass and moss; the 'roof' consists of dried leaves and other plant matter. In winter the hedgehog might build a larger nest, cushioned and covered with dried leaves. The roof is often very thick to make the nest waterproof. The winter nest can be constructed the same way as in summer but is often in a more protected place, for example, in a hollow tree or abandoned Rabbit burrow; a Western Hedgehog will hibernate the entire winter in this nest.

Hedgehogs have long whiskers. Biopix.

You often find Western Hedgehog nests in large piles of brushwood. LG.

Algerian Hedgehogs have larger ears and a lighter coat and spines than Western Hedgehogs.

Algerian Hedgehog

Erinaceus algirus

Algerian Hedgehog has longer legs than Western Hedgehog, and the quills on its head are separated by an area of no spines. It has larger ears, and the coat and spines are lighter than those of Western Hedgehog. It is found in similar habitats but is restricted in distribution to small areas of France and Spain. It also leaves tracks similar to those of Western Hedgehog; however, it does not hibernate.

Common Shrew

Sorex araneus

The Common Shrew is the most abundant shrew species in Europe. It feeds on insects and invertebrates, particularly earthworms. Common Shrew is a little smaller than Water Shrew; it is 5.5–8.5 cm long, with a 3–5.5 cm tail, and it weighs 4–16 g. As is the case with other shrew species, the head is elongated and narrow and has long feeler hairs.

Common Shrews are tricoloured, with a reddish brown back, a greyish white belly, and a third, transitional colour between these two areas. The tail is covered with short hairs and dark on the upper side and light on the underside.

Common Shrews are small, active animals that can live only a few hours without food. They feed mostly on earthworms, insects and their larvae, snails, and also some carrion and may also eat plant seeds.

Common Shrews can live anywhere dense vegetation grows. They live in territories they defend from competitors, and you can sometimes hear the fierce cries of battling shrews as they compete over a territory. Common Shrews are active year-round.

On soft terrain, for example mud near a puddle, you can see Common Shrew tracks. Mice have only four toes on their

Common Shrews jump in the snow.

Common Shrews like earthworms. LG.

front feet, while Common Shrew has five toes on both front and hind feet. The front footprint is 8–9 mm long and wide; the hind footprint, 10 mm long and wide. The tail drag marks may also be visible in mud.

Shrews usually walk. The stride is about 4 cm, but these animals can also jump forward, and then the distance between prints is about 5 cm. The front footprints are always in front of the hind.

Common Shrews move on the ground between plants along very narrow trails and in the tunnel systems of other animals. They also dig their own tunnels immediately under the surface, where they might be found, mainly in winter. The entrances are very small, at the most the diameter of an index finger, about 2.2 cm. The tracks

of a Common Shrew moving in snow will usually lead to an entrance hole.

In the tunnel system small chambers are prepared with leaves, moss, and grass, in which the animals rest. The female's nest is a little larger than a rest chamber and very compact. Common Shrew's scat is very small, 2.4 mm long and 1–2 mm thick, often pointed at both ends; and it can be found beneath roots, stones, etc.

Common Shrew is tricoloured. LG.

Other shrews. Many species of shrew are found in Europe. The tracks of these species, apart from some size differences, are almost impossible to distinguish from each other. Only Common Shrew has a tricoloured coat.

Shrews are the smallest mammals in Europe. The **Pygmy Shrew** is 4–6 cm long, with a 3–4.5 cm tail, and it weighs only 2.5–7.5 g. The **Pygmy White-toothed Shrew** weighs just 2 g.

Dead shrews. You rarely find small dead mammals in the wild, because they are soon eaten by other animals. This is not the case with shrews, whose bodies you encounter quite frequently. The reason is that shrews have glands on either side of their bodies that secrete a substance smelling strongly of musk, which many predators find distasteful. Shrews are often confused with other rodents and killed by

You often find dead shrews in the wild. Here, a Pygmy Shrew. AK.

predators, but the bodies are left behind as inedible.

Eurasian Badgers eat shrews, as do various birds, shrikes, skuas, and owls, in particular. Boreal Owls and Barn Owls prey on shrews; for these species, the shrews may make up half their diet. Short-eared Owls and Long-eared Owls also eat many shrews.

Pygmy Shrews live in dense vegetation; here you can also see the winter nest, which becomes visible after snow has melted. In winter they may also use buildings. Pygmy Shrews are better at jumping than other shrew species. AK.

Bats are rarely seen during the day. AK.

Bats

About 30 species of bats are resident in Europe, and it is practically impossible to tell them apart from their tracks. They are all nocturnal and catch insects in flight; all species hibernate.

During the day they roost in attics, cellars, holes in rocks, caves, hollow trees, woodpecker cavities, nest boxes, bat boxes, and other quiet places; they also hibernate at many of the same sites.

If you are lucky you might find bat tracks on the ground, for example, on muddy shores or wet woodland paths. The hind foot of a bat has five toes with powerful claws that leave clear marks. The 'thumbs' on the wing leave only a single mark, normally visible on each side of the footprints and outside them. The drag marks of the tail might be visible between the footprints.

Below bat roosts and their entrance holes you may find the remains of prey, for example beetle wings, often in large quantities.

Below roost sites you will also find scat resembling that of mice, but a bat's is not as smooth and round, though it will always appear shiny because it contains

A Parti-coloured Bat hangs upside down. LG.

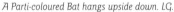

The Parti-coloured Bat walks with the help of claws on the wings and legs. LG.

insect remains. Scat is dark brown to black and very porous and can often be found in large piles. It is 2–8 mm long and 2–3 mm thick.

The floor of the roost site can acquire a dark colouration from the bats' urine and scat.

Beware! Bats can spread deadly diseases like rabies, and for this reason you should never touch them; if you are bitten by a bat, immediately seek medical attention.

A Parti-coloured Bat with spread wings, the claw on the wing clearly visible. LG.

When bats walk, they hold their wings close to the body. When moving faster, they extend their wings.

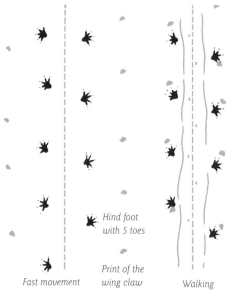

Hind foot with 5 toes

Fast movement

Print of the wing claw

Walking

Horses

Equus caballus

The horse is a highly specialised mammal, adapted to living on grassland and plains where it can move at great speed. The second and fourth toes are completely missing; thus all four feet have only one toe, equivalent to the third toe of other mammal species. Horses step on the outermost part of the foot and have a distinctive hoof enclosing a small pad.

The footprints are essentially circular and cannot be confused with other tracks when the animal is wearing horseshoes. Since horses are heavy animals, the prints are easily recognisable. Depending on the size of the horse and the speed it is moving, the prints can be between 12 and 25 cm in diameter.

If the horse is unshod, the hooves will leave a large circular print with a deep

Horse scat

V-shaped notch towards the rear. Horse scat is spherical and about 3–5 cm in diameter. The scat is brownish and contains undigested plant remains, especially grass stems. In the wild, birds and insects feed on whatever nutrients remain in the scat.

Horse. Biopix. Inset: A print with (left) and without a horseshoe. Left, EHA; right, KG.

Cattle

Bos taurus

Cattle, like deer, have two toes. so their tracks can be confused with those of deer, especially Elk. But cattle normally graze together in meadows, so you will always find numerous tracks in one place; they also trample distinct rutted paths in fields and meadows.

The size and shape of tracks vary greatly according to breed. Overall, they are broad and round, on average 10–12 cm long and 9–10 cm wide. The single hoof is concave at the front and convex at the back; you normally cannot see both toes in the footprints.

Elk footprints are usually more pointed, somewhat larger, and the stride is also longer; moreover, elk are solitary and their tracks would not be restricted by a fence line.

Cattle scat, 'cowpat', is dark brown and very moist when fresh. It is found as a plate-sized flat pile but quickly dries to a light brown or greyish mound.

A cowpat with holes from insects that have emerged. NPHH.

Many insects lay eggs in cowpats. When the insects emerge from the larval stage, they bore through the edge of the cowpat, leaving small circular holes.

Insect larvae and worms attract many predators to cowpats: Carrion Crows, Rooks, Starlings, and Curlews will forage in cowpats for larvae and worms; Western Hedgehogs can completely tear them apart when foraging, and Eurasian Badgers will flip them over in the hunt for a meal.

Cow tracks never show the imprint of the dew claw. AK; inset, EHA.

Wild Boar

Sus scrofa

The Wild Boar is a powerfully built animal with a compact body and large triangular head. It has strong legs and can run fast. The female, a sow, can weigh 55–100 kg; the male, the boar, is larger and normally weighs 65–150 kg, but an old male can weigh more than 200 kg. The height at the shoulder is 85–100 cm.

Wild Boar prefer mixed deciduous woodland with swamps and water holes, often with a mix of fields, meadows, or moorland nearby. Sows and young live in herds; the males are solitary except during the mating season in winter. Wild Boar have long, sharp canines in the lower jaw that can reach 20 cm in length and protrude well out of the mouth.

The young have a light brown coat with dark stripes; adults and juveniles are dark grey.

Wild Boar feed mainly on plants, mushrooms, roots, bulbs, grain, maize, acorns, beechnuts, and chestnuts as well as fruit;

Baby Wild Boar are striped. Biopix.

they also eat worms, snails, insects, and larvae, as well as mice and other rodents. They also plunder bird nests on the ground and feed on carrion as well as killing fawns and young Rabbits.

Wild Boar can cause extensive damage to fields when they root for food or eat crops such as maize, oats, turnips, and potatoes.

The powerful canines of a large male Wild Boar. LG.

Wild Boar scat smells sweetish. L-HO.

Wild Boar tracks with the print of the dew claw visible in mud at a wallow. JK.

Wild Boar have hooves like deer. They have four toes; the middle two are large, while the two dew claws are much smaller but normally visible in footprints irrespective of the animal's gait. In older individuals, the large hooves have rounded edges. In footprints, you can see that the dew claws are placed more laterally and closer together in Wild Boar than in deer. In adults the print is 5–8 cm long and 4–6 cm wide; deer tracks are narrower and more elongated. The stride is 20–40 cm, but Wild Boar will switch quickly from walking to running.

Wild Boar herds are often led by an old sow. You can identify the herd's tracks quite easily, especially in the snow, and see where members of the herd have followed one another in a line. With their strong snouts

Wild Boar can root up ground so badly with their snouts that crop cultivation is not possible. AK.

Wild Boar do not kill large animals themselves, but they gladly feed on carrion—here an Elk. L-HO.

Wild Boar root through the top layers of soil looking for snails, roots, worms, and insect larvae, and in the process may plough up extensive areas. These tracks are clear evidence of Wild Boar activity.

The scat is sausage-shaped, 7 cm thick and about 10 cm long. It is normally found in cohesive clumps, similar to the summer scat of deer. The scat is black but may turn grey after a while.

Wild Boar love to wallow in mud and water to rid themselves of irritating

Wild Boar are very shy, but they can sometimes be surprised out in the open. PFM.

A herd goosesteps through deep snow.

parasites and to protect their skin from biting insects. You often see prints and scat at these wallows. There is usually a strong, distinct smell of the animal at a recently used wallow.

When a boar has wallowed, it rubs itself on large stones or nearby trees. The tree trunk may then appear completely smooth (*cf*. p. 53). Occasionally, marks from their canine teeth or long, greyish black hair might also be found.

Wild Boar are mostly nocturnal; during the day they lie in well-hidden rest sites on the forest floor that may be cushioned with grass and leaves.

A pregnant sow prepares a large nest with grass stalks, ferns, and branches for the time when she will give birth; initially she raises the young, but after a few weeks, they can feed independently and follow her in the forest.

Wild Boar are animals of the forest. PFM.

Elk

Alces alces

Elk are the largest species of deer in Europe, and on account of their size alone cannot be confused with other animals. The coat is dark brown to almost completely black; the legs are lighter, especially in females. The ears are large and mobile.

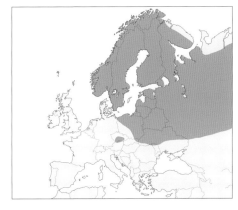

A full-grown female can reach a height at the shoulder of 170–180 cm, the male about 180–220 cm; Elk are 2–3 m in length, and the relatively short tail is about 10 cm long. There is a slight hump on the back. The large upper lip juts over the lower jaw, and a fold of skin hangs below the neck, covered with long hairs. An adult female can weigh 340–400 kg, an adult male, 380–500 kg, but in the northernmost regions, just before the mating season in September/October, up to 1 ton. The male's antlers are set at an angle of almost 90 degrees from the head, with the palmations pointing upwards.

Elk live in open conifer forest, particularly with scattered deciduous trees, extensive ground vegetation, and accessible water nearby. They are most active from dusk until dawn.

In summer, Elk feed on leaves and young branches of willows, sorbs, ashes, birches, and oaks, as well as plants such as willow-herbs, meadowsweet, water lilies, and other succulent aquatic plants. In autumn they eat bell heather and blueberries, apples, wild oats, and other kinds of cereal. Elk may also look for food in fields of rape, clover, and peas. In winter they eat mostly pine needles, the branches of young pine and deciduous

A female Elk with a large calf. LGA.

trees, and the bark of wild service tree, ash, and pine.

Elk tracks are distinctive in practically all types of terrain; they are 12–16 cm long and about 13 cm wide; the female's footprints are smaller than those of the male. The dew claw is positioned lower on the hoof than in other deer, with the exception of Reindeer.

On soft terrain you can often make out the mark of the dew claws. The footprints may be significantly splayed, and the stride is 150–200 cm. Elk tracks are larger than those of other deer but somewhat

An Elk footprint with the dew claw distinctly visible. LG.

similar to cattle tracks. A female's hooves are not as pointed, and overall her tracks are shorter and more rounded, and may not show the imprint of the dew claw. The footprints of Red Deer are smaller, while those of Reindeer are more rounded.

Elk feed on small pine branches up to a height of 3 m; larger branches may be broken and left hanging. The chewed branches have frayed edges. In order to reach branches higher up, Elk press down on a tree trunk with their chest, and sometimes the tree breaks under the pressure. Elk leave very powerful gnaw marks on bark, especially on European aspen. You can see the distinct marks of the lower teeth; they leave wide grooves running up the trunk (*cf.* p. 47), as if the work of a carpenter, and these can reach to about 2.5 m.

Elk scat is easily identified based on its shape and size. It is left in piles, and the individual segments are round and roughly the shape of a large grape. The scat can be slightly fatter at one end and is 2– 3 cm long and 1.5–2 cm wide. In summer the

Elk tracks in deep snow. JT.

Elk summer scat. EHA.

Normal Elk scat. AK.

scat is very dark, almost black, and soft. If Elk eat a lot of succulent plants, the 'grapes' can merge to form a somewhat indistinct mass resembling a cowpat. In the winter the 'grapes' are lighter and harder, since they consist mostly of large fibres.

In both summer and winter, you can find areas where Elk have settled down to ruminate. In summer the grass is trampled

In winter, Elk eat large numbers of spruce needles. BW.

in a 1 m radius around a rest area, but a rest area is most easily identified in snow or a heavy frost, and the animal's scat will often be found nearby.

In August and September, the Elk rubs the velvet off its new antlers, using young trees and larger bushes. During this process, branches can break off, and the bark can hang in strips.

During the mating season, from the end of September to the beginning of October, the male uses his feet to create a hollow in the ground 1–1.5 m wide in which he urinates. When it rains, these rutting pits can become stinking sloughs in which the Elk lies and rubs mud into his coat. Females and one-year old calves may also wallow in the mud.

Elk are highly mobile, especially young males. They often use the same trails in the forest, which can be completely trampled down after time. When Elk pass near barbed wire fences, you can often find long greyish brown hairs caught on the fence.

Above: The body heat of an Elk has melted a thin layer of snow in its rest area. L-HO.
Below: A male Elk, the dream of every hunter. TF.

Red Deer

Cervus elaphus

Red Deer is the second largest deer species in Europe; only Elk is larger. The female, the doe, is smaller than the male. Female Red Deer are slightly less than 2 m in length, and weigh 60–120 kg. The stag is slightly more than 2 m long and weighs, on average, 140–150 kg, but can weigh up to 240 kg.

Red Deer are 120–140 cm tall at the shoulder, with a tail about 15 cm long. The coat is yellowish brown, but in the area around the tail is a light reddish yellow.

An adult Red Deer in dense woodland. ME.

Red Deer have a reddish brown coat on the upperparts with a variable dark stripe along the back; the belly is whitish yellow. The winter coat is greyish brown and has longer, thicker hair. Older stags develop a mane of hair around the neck. From summer to spring, adult deer have a large, branched set of antlers with a forked 'crown' in the middle.

Red Deer live in herds in open woodland near fields, and also inhabit

A younger male with does in dunes. SS.

Red Deer tracks with imprints of the dew claws. LG.

If undisturbed, Red Deer move with a stride of about 1 m, and the hind foot is often placed in the print of the forefoot. If the animals feel threatened, they trot with a stride of about 3 m, or may even gallop and jump. The tracks of the hooves show evenly curved outer edges; the toe pads measure only one-third the hoof's length.

Does' hooves are 6–7 cm long and 4.5–5 cm wide, the stags' 8–9 cm long and 6–7 cm wide, with a more rounded tip than those of the female, and the males' footprints are sometimes more oblique. The outer part of the hoof is a little larger in the footprint than the inside. The prints of the front hooves are the largest and the most distinctly splayed. The faster the animal moves, the further apart the hoof prints. Where the tracks are clear on soft terrain or in the snow, you can see the imprints of the dew claws, especially those of the front hooves. The doe's stride is 90–110 cm, the stag's, 110–150 cm.

Red Deer footprints are the same size as those of an Elk calf, but the latter are more pointed at the front. Fallow Deer footprints are narrower and also more pointed at the front. Wild Boar footprints

heathland and upland areas. The does and their calves live separately until the mating season in September/October, while the other adults gather in smaller groups. You will normally see Red Deer at dusk or early in the morning.

During the rut, male Red Deer engage in combat. LG.

are wider than those of Red Deer and the stride significantly shorter; also, the dew claws can be seen more distinctly. Goat and sheep tracks may resemble those of Red Deer but are also significantly shorter. Herds of Red Deer often move in long columns, with only a few individuals side by side. In some regions like Norway and Scotland, Red Deer move from upland

Red Deer tracks in sand. PB.

Red Deer tracks

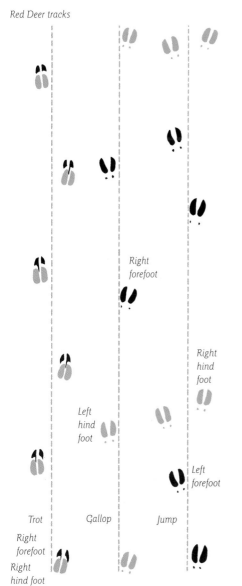

Right forefoot

Right hind foot

Left hind foot

Left forefoot

Trot

Gallop

Jump

Right forefoot

Right hind foot

Red Deer scat. PB.

as single droppings or in small quantities where the animals have been walking. In summer the scat more or less coheres and may resemble a small irregular cowpat.

Red Deer eat a lot of grass and other plants such as heather and blueberries; in summer, the leaves of trees and bushes as well as lichens and mushrooms are also grazed. They can consume crops such as rape and clover and may also unearth potatoes. In coastal areas they also eat seaweed. In zoos, or when in large groups, they can defoliate trees as far up as they can reach.

In winter they eat the shoots of conifers, deciduous trees, and bushes. Since they have no incisors, the chewed-off branches are frayed. Small trees can be deformed by deer feeding, until the tree grows beyond a height subject to such damage. Spruces can develop a thick, conical shape at their base as a result of frequent grazing (cf. p. 48).

Red Deer love turnips and will often pull young plants out of the ground to take just one or a few bites from each. They eat only the above-ground parts of a ripe turnip, in the process leaving distinct, wide grooves with their large lower front teeth.

In spring Red Deer peel the bark from young conifers, often removing large pieces

areas, which they frequent during summer, to lower-lying regions in the winter, and then move back up the following summer. During these seasonal movements, they follow specific, clearly marked trails.

The fresh scat of Red Deer is black and slick, later becoming dark brown and dull. The scat is cylindrical, 2–2.5 cm long and 1.3–1.8 cm thick, and may be finely pointed at one end, with a small hole at the other end.

Red Deer scat is somewhat smaller than Elk's and slightly larger than that of Fallow Deer. Scat is normally found in small piles in areas where the animals have stopped to eat or ruminate, but it can also be found

A rutting Red Deer. LG.

Gnaw marks on a cast-off antler. LG.

A wallow.

or strips. If the bark is removed all the way around the trunk, the tree can die. If, in winter, the bark is still firmly attached to the tree, the marks of the lower front teeth can be seen as distinctive grooves on the bark; they are about 4–5 cm wide and often follow the vertical axis of the trunk. When a tree has been extensively grazed, it may survive only if the bark grows back.

Fallow and Sika Deer also feed on trees; the marks of the two species are difficult to separate. Elk gnaw marks are deeper and found higher on a tree.

An adult Red Deer has very large antlers. When they are fully grown in August, they remove the velvet by rubbing the antlers against bushes and young trees; in the process, branches are broken off, and the remains of velvet are visible up to a height of 120 cm. The deer may also rub against larger trees, and in so doing heavily mark the bark. It's hard to find rubbed-off velvet since the deer usually eat it. During the mating season, deer also rub their antlers on trees. The antlers are shed in early spring, between February and May.

Red Deer like bathing and are good swimmers. In summer and autumn, they also wallow in mud along lake shores and on moors and even use small puddles, for example, pools formed by vehicle tracks. Red Deer rub off the mud against trees, which over time become smooth, and you will find hair on the trees and on ground nearby.

During the mating season, a Red Deer will scratch a hollow in the ground, an arena for rutting, in which it rolls the same way an Elk or Fallow Deer would. The hollow will acquire the powerful smell of a stag's urine and semen. Near the hollow you will find trees on which the animal has rubbed itself. The rut occurs between the end of September and the beginning of October, a little before that of Sika Deer and about a month prior to the rut of Fallow Deer.

Damage to a fir tree caused by deer rubbing. LG.

White-tailed Deer

White-tailed Deer with doe. TLA.

Odocoileus virginianus

White-tailed Deer have a reddish brown coat with a whitish throat and belly. The inside of the ears is white, and there is a white ring around the eyes and snout. White-tailed Deer are a little larger than Fallow Deer and somewhat smaller than Red Deer; they measure 90–105 cm at the shoulder, weigh 50–135 kg, and are about 115–170 cm long, with a relatively long tail of 15–28 cm, which is brownish above and white below. When running, the animal raises its tail, and the white area on the underside becomes visible.

The stag is larger than the doe. The antlers have three or four crowns, and they are shed each December.

White-tailed Deer are very much tied to specific locales and can often be seen at woodland edges where there is access to fields, also in larger clearings. They prefer deciduous forest near open fields but will forage for food in agricultural land. They may also visit gardens. They feed on shoots and leaves of deciduous trees, but also graze on conifers. In summer they live in small family herds, and in winter in larger groups of up to 25 individuals. If threatened, they sometimes stomp the ground and emit a baying sound.

White-tailed Deer are native to North America. They were introduced into Finland in 1934, where there is now a large population in the southern part of the country; otherwise, apart from those in zoos and deer parks, smaller populations reside in the Czech Republic, Serbia, and Croatia.

The footprint is elongated and narrow and resembles that of a Fallow Deer; it is about 7 cm long and 4 cm wide, and may be splayed. The stride is about 90 cm; when the animal is galloping, the stride increases and can reach 180 cm or more in length.

The scat resembles that of Fallow and Red Deer, each individual 'grape' about 1.5–2.5 cm long and 1–1.5 cm wide.

Fallow Deer
Cervus dama

Fallow Deer prefer open deciduous and mixed forest with clearings and luxuriant underbrush, often near fields and grassland. Fallow Deer are 130–160 cm long, with a 20 cm tail, which is longer than that of other deer species. The area around the tail is white and demarcated above and on the sides by a clear black border. Fallow Deer measure 85–110 cm at the shoulder; the doe is smaller than the stag. The doe weighs 30–50 kg, the stag, 60–110 kg. At the start of the summer, adult deer have large, shovel-shaped antlers, which are ultimately shed in April/May.

Surrounding the genitals, Fallow Deer have a distinct tuft of hair. In summer the Fallow Deer's coat is reddish brown above with numerous white spots, the underside is light brown, and there is a black stripe along the back, continuing all the way to the tip of the tail. In winter the stag is greyish brown above with blurred spots. The coats of Fallow Deer can be variably coloured; in summer they can be quite dark and without spots, or almost completely white, and many individuals fall on a spectrum somewhere between light and dark.

Fallow Deer live in herds the same way Red Deer do, though herds of Fallow Deer are looser. The stags form smaller groups or are solitary.

Fallow Deer are active mostly in the morning and evening, but if undisturbed, might also be seen during the day, like Red Deer.

Footprints are small and round, more elongated than those of Red Deer. An individual print has a sharp point and is narrow, the sides being almost parallel. The pads are large and half as long as the hoof. The doe's footprint is 5–6 cm long and 3–3.5 cm wide, the stag's, 6–8 cm long

During the mating season, Fallow Deer fight doggedly. LG.

The distinctive tail area of a Fallow Deer. Biopix.

have a shorter step; Red Deer footprints are larger, longer, and wider.

Sika Deer footprints resemble those of Fallow Deer, but are wider, and the feet are noticeably splayed. Tracks of domestic sheep also resemble those of Fallow Deer but are rounder and wider, and sheep never leave tracks with dew claws.

Fallow Deer feed on grass and plants, but also eat the leaves of trees and bushes and crops such as clover, and they also feed on berries, beechnuts, and acorns. The scat of Fallow Deer is similar to that of Red Deer but smaller, about 1–2 cm long and 0.8–1.2 cm thick, often thicker at one end and pointed at the other. The clumps are smaller than those made by Red Deer, and slightly larger than those of Roe Deer. Unlike Red Deer scat, especially in summer, that of Fallow Deer is found in relatively well-formed piles.

and 4–5 cm wide. On soft terrain and in snow, the dew claws are clearly visible in the print. The stride is 70–100 cm. The tracks of Roe Deer are smaller, and Roe

An adult Fallow Deer and a footprint in mud. AK; inset, LG.

As with other species, Fallow Deer can damage young trees and bushes by rubbing their antlers against them to rub off velvet; this usually occurs between July and the end of September.

Fallow Deer will also peel the bark off trees. The marks of grazing by Fallow Deer are at a lower height on the tree and usually on thinner trunks than Elk would use, but at the same height as those left by Red Deer; the tooth marks of a Fallow are smaller. In spring, Fallow Deer tear off long strips of bark, a behaviour you can quite easily see when they are in captivity.

Like Red Deer, Fallow scrape hollows for rutting but often place them much closer together. The Fallow Deer rut season lasts from October to early November.

Fallow Deer scat. LG.

Tracks of a Fallow Deer herd, as well as those of a hare and a fox. LG.

Sika Deer

Cervus nippon

Sika Deer were introduced to Europe from eastern Asia in the mid-nineteenth century. They are medium-sized, smaller and more slender than Fallow Deer, but larger than Roe Deer. They are 120–140 cm long, with a 10–15 cm tail. At the shoulder they measure 80–85 cm. The female weighs 28–40 kg, the stag 40–55 kg. Sika Deer have small and minimally branched antlers with a maximum of 4 points (ends) on each branch. The antlers are shed each year in April/May; the velvet on new antlers is rubbed off in August/September.

In summer a Sika Deer's coat is reddish brown with variably marked longitudinal rows of light spots, and a black stripe runs along the back; in winter the animal is dark greyish brown. On the back of the hind legs, directly under the tail, is an almost pure white spot.

This spot resembles that found on Fallow Deer, but the black 'frame' is less pronounced, and a Sika's tail has only a narrow black stripe on the upper side. When Sika Deer run, they raise the hair around this white spot; it is then clearly visible.

Sika Deer are similar to Red Deer in behaviour, but Sika's rut lasts longer, from September to the beginning of December. Sika Deer live in dense woodland with underbrush and clearings, close to fields. Like Red and Fallow Deer, they rub the bark off trees. The scat is similar to that of Red and Roe Deer, but usually found in one spot.

The tracks of Sika Deer are similar to those of Fallow Deer but broader, and the feet are more markedly splayed.

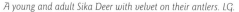

A young and adult Sika Deer with velvet on their antlers. LG.

Reeve's Muntjac
Muntiacus reevesi

Reeve's Muntjac is a relatively small and compact species, introduced to some European countries from Southeast Asia. The deer vocalize quite loudly and for this reason are also known as Barking Deer.

Muntjac are light brown on the back and sides and light coloured on the inside of the legs, and they have a light-coloured spot in the area around the tail, visible only when the tail is raised. They have a black V-shaped marking on the face, from the rear of the nose to the pedicles of the antlers. The buck has small, fork-shaped antlers that rise from long pedicles and also sports a pair of significantly prolonged, sharp canines (tusks) in the upper jaw, protruding visibly from the mouth.

Muntjac are about 95 cm long, with a 10 cm tail, measure 40–65 cm at the shoulder, and weigh about 15–35 kg.

Reeve's Muntjac live in deciduous and mixed woodland, preferably with a dense underbrush, and are solitary. They feed on twigs and branches of trees and bushes, but normally do not peel the bark off. They are mainly nocturnal.

Muntjac tracks are easy to recognise, since the footprints are not symmetrical and the inner hoof is less clearly marked

A Reeve's Muntjac with long pedicles and a black V-shaped mark on its forehead. DK.

A Muntjac doe. The yellowish brown spot under the tail is visible when the tail is raised. DT.

than the outer. The tracks are up to 3 cm long; the prints of the dew claw can be seen only in very soft terrain. The stride is 25–30 cm.

The scat is black and almost circular, about 1 cm thick. The scat is normally scattered widely and in large quantities where the animal has fed on plants in the underbrush, but it might also be found in cohesive clumps.

Muntjac tracks with scat.

Roe Deer

Capreolus capreolus

Roe Deer is one of the smallest deer in Europe, 95–135 cm long, with a 2–4 cm tail, mostly obscured by the coat. It is 65–75 cm at the shoulder, and males are larger than females. In much of Europe, Roe Deer weigh 20–25 kg; in northern Scandinavia, they can weigh up to 35 kg.

The summer coat is reddish brown on the sides and back, the belly somewhat lighter. The winter coat is greyish brown and significantly thicker; the coat of some Roe Deer can be dark brown, almost black. The buck has small antlers, two branches with three pointed ends each, once the animal is two years old. The antlers grow in the spring and are shed in November/December.

Roe Deer live in open woodland with thick underbrush and in clearings, with open farm fields or uncultivated areas nearby. They are active at dusk and dawn, but in summer, if undisturbed, can be active all day.

The tracks are 4–5 cm long and 3 cm wide, those of younger individuals more pointed; the tracks of older deer are rounded. There are no differences between the prints of bucks and does. The footprints are almost parallel, with the splaying more pronounced at increased running speeds; the prints of the front feet are V-shaped. If the animals run very fast, you can also

Roe Deer have white around the tail. IK.

Roe Deer dig under the snow for plants. Inset: A track in snow with the prints of dew claws. PB.

see the imprints of the dew claws, and the same is true when the animal moves over soft terrain. The stride is 60–90 cm.

When moving at a leisurely gait, a Roe Deer places its hind feet in the prints of the front; when running, it often places the hind feet ahead of the front. In flight, or when galloping, the hind feet are set outside and significantly ahead of the front footprints.

An adult buck with velvet on its antlers. ME.

The tracks of Wild Boar are wider and heavier, and those of Fallow Deer, longer and narrower.

Roe Deer often use the same trails between hiding places in the woods and from one field to another; frequently other animals use these paths as well, and as a result, the trails become well trodden. In snow these trails are easily seen, and you can also find depressions in the snow where deer hide during the day.

Adult bucks lay claim to a territory from May to September, marking it with both scat and secretions from glands on their forehead and between their hooves. To mark territory, the buck rubs its forehead against small trees and bushes and simultaneously scratches the ground with its front feet. Bark and small branches are ripped off small trees, and you can also find long rub marks made by antlers. You see the same rub marks from the end of March to the middle of April, when the buck uses small trees and

Roe Deer tracks in a field and in sand. LG; inset, LJ.

bushes to remove the velvet from its antlers. The trees involved are normally no more than 2 cm in diameter. The buck sheds its antlers between October and December.

Roe Deer does give birth in May. The fawns are spotted for the first few months of their lives. MDDH.

Roe Deer bucks rub their antlers on young trees and large bushes. LG.

A Roe Deer's territorial markings. AK.

In summer Roe Deer feed on plants, but they are quite picky. They strongly favour certain plants, for instance, anemones. These animals also like polyantha roses and fallen fruit, especially apples, and may also consume mushrooms.

In winter Roe Deer eat all the green plants they can find and also graze on heather and blueberries as well as buds and branches of trees and bushes, especially hazel, oaks, poplars, and spruce. Roe Deer do not normally gnaw on bark the way larger deer species do, but in the case of a young spruce, they might feed on the tallest shoots and many of the lower branches. The gnawing of a Roe Deer, unlike that of a hare, leaves clear fray marks (*cf.* p. 62). A

young tree with lower branches grazed will develop new ones and become very dense in the regenerated areas. You can see also this phenomenon in young oaks.

Roe Deer scat is cylindrical, 10–16 mm long and 7–10 mm thick, black or dark brown, slightly pointed at one end, and rounded at the other. In summer, Roe Deer can leave scat in large, more or less cohesive clumps, but normally scat will be scattered. The deer also defecates while walking, so you can find individual clumps between footprints.

When ruminating or resting, Roe Deer normally lie on the ground. Unlike other deer species, Roe clear away any leaves or branches and occasionally even the vegetation itself before lying down. The resting

Roe Deer scat in summer. LG.

Roe Deer scat in October. LG.

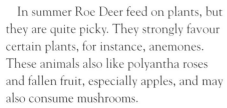

A Roe Deer 'fairy ring'. LG.

area is about 60 cm long and 40 cm wide, and you will find plentiful scat nearby.

In summer, bucks usually move to an area that may also be home to several does. The does stay with their offspring from the previous year up to the next mating season, the end of July to August, then chase the young away. When a buck meets a doe ready to mate, it will often follow her closely during the one-day rutting period. Shortly before mating, the doe runs around in a tight circle, closely pursued by the buck. As a result, circular trails are formed in the plant cover, and these are called 'fairy rings'.

Young Roe Deer. JKK.

Reindeer
Rangifer tarandus

Truly wild Reindeer are now very rare, with only one significant population in the Hardangervidda of the Dovrefjell-Rondane region in Norway, some small populations in Finland, as well as a population of 'wood' Reindeer, a long-legged race, in eastern Finland; the remaining wild populations have interbred almost completely with domesticated animals.

Reindeer have a dark, greyish brown coat in summer, which becomes lighter in

Reindeer proceed in goosestep fashion in deep snow to conserve energy. Inset: Small tracks in snow, Biopix.

winter. The belly is white, and the tail and surrounding area are also white. The front part of the body including the neck beard is whitish.

Reindeer are 185–220 cm long, 90–110 cm high at the shoulder; the female weighs 40–100 kg, the stag is larger and weighs 70–150 kg; the tail is 10–15 cm long.

Both sexes have antlers, though the stag's are larger. A few individuals may lack antlers. Stags rub off the antler velvet in August/September; the doe sheds her antlers in May.

Reindeer live in large herds; in summer in Scandinavia, they stay in the high mountains, while in autumn they move to wooded areas at lower elevations.

The tracks can be confused with those of Musk Ox. A single footprint is kidney-shaped, 8–10 cm long but wider than that of an Ox. The does' footprints are smaller and more pointed.

The dew claws are large and positioned somewhat lower on the foot than is the case with Elk and other deer species. Prints of the dew claws, especially those

on the front feet, which are more noticeably splayed, are always visible in tracks on soft terrain and in snow.

In the tracks, hind footprints partially or completely cover the front footprints. The stride is 90–120 cm. Reindeer usually move slowly, but if they feel threatened they run, and the stride is then 120–200 cm. Reindeer seldom jump or gallop flat out, though they are very fast when they do.

Reindeer follow particular routes in their wanderings, and they often walk in a long line behind an older doe. These routes can be seen as distinctively trodden trails.

In summer, Reindeer feed on grass and plants, the leaves of small trees and bushes, mushrooms, and lichens. A specific kind of lichen is named after the animal, reindeer-moss (*Cladonia rangiferina*). In winter they prefer lichens, which they dig for under the snow, and the deep holes they excavate are very distinctive. If snow is too deep or too hard for them to dig, the Reindeer eat lichens growing on trees, when

Wild Reindeer in the Hardangervidda in Norway. TF.

The scat comprises small hard balls.

Reindeer track with the imprint of the dew claw. LG.

you can see their tracks running from tree to tree. Reindeer do not eat bark.

When the snow has melted in spring, you will find large areas in a wood where lichens, moss, and small bushes have been completely consumed.

Reindeer scat is similar to that of Roe Deer, and somewhat smaller than sheep scat. In winter, the balls are small and

A small herd of wild Reindeer wander far and wide in winter looking for food. AK.

twisted, 1–1.5 cm long and 0.5–1 cm thick, often slightly flattened on the sides and with a small point at one end. In spring and autumn, scat is dark brown, softer, and more cohesive. In summer, the scat can meld together and look like a cowpat, with a diameter of about 10 cm.

Reindeer rub the velvet off their antlers before the rutting season, which lasts from late September to early October. They rub on small trees, often spruce, frequently peeling off the bark. You can sometimes find remains of the velvet on the trees if lucky.

In summer, when the animals lose their thick coat, you will find tufts of coarse, wavy hair.

Musk Ox

Ovibos moschatus

Musk Ox is a polar animal, introduced from northeastern Greenland to the Dovrefjell-Rondane region of Norway, from which it has expanded into the Härje valley in Sweden.

It is related to sheep and goats and has a compact body with a small hump above the shoulders, a large, wide head, large dark eyes, and small pointed ears, almost completely covered by fur. The tail is very small and covered by fur.

The animal is covered with coarse hair, up to 50 cm long, that reaches its feet; beneath this it has a lighter, softer under-coat that can be spun into threads like sheep's wool. Musk Ox is dark brown with large white spots on its back and lighter-coloured legs, snout, and forehead. The snout is hairy, and the fur reaches even below the hooves.

Musk Ox is 1.8–2.3 m long, 1.2–1.5 m at the shoulder, and weighs 200–350 kg; the male is larger.

Both sexes have large horns, which are broader and rougher at the base. In old males, the horns can cover the entire fore-head; females have a light, hair-covered area between the horns. The horns point down-wards and forward and have pointed tips.

Musk Oxen live in herds. During the mating season, from August to October, the sexually mature bulls fight for females; in the process, the dominant bull banishes the others. The bulls stand with lowered heads

When it's too warm, female Musk Oxen gladly rest in snow. AK.

Musk Ox hair can often be found on bushes and trees. LG.

Musk Ox tracks in mud. LG.

facing each other and ram the opponent's head with such force that clashes echo in surrounding mountains. In May or June, the cow gives birth to a calf, more rarely two, and cares for it for 18 months; a calf becomes sexually mature at 4 years of age.

The tracks can be confused with those of Reindeer. Musk Ox footprints are almost circular, and the single hoof print is kidney-shaped, 8–11 cm long. The hooves are somewhat asymmetrical, since the outer hoof is slightly larger and rounder than the inner, which is a little more pointed. The stride is 80–120 cm, and the legs are splayed far more than is the case with Reindeer.

You will get to see prints of dew claws only in deep snow, and they are closer together than in a Reindeer footprint. If threatened, Musk Oxen will run very fast, with a stride between 2.5 and 3.5 m; the hoofs are not splayed when running.

The animals feed on young willow shoots, grass, herbs, moss, and lichens. Their scat lies in small mounds and resembles that of Reindeer, but is somewhat larger, slick, and more oval, 1.5–2 cm long and about 1 cm thick. In summer the scat is more cohesive and more angular in shape.

You almost always find scat together with some of the animal's long hair. Musk Oxen lose a good portion of their coat in summer, and you can find large tufts of the undercoat on the ground or in bushes and trees.

Beware! Musk Oxen are very shy when interacting with humans, but you should still keep a safe distance. If the herd gathers in a semicircular formation, and the bulls begin to snort, stamp on the ground, or tear up plants and stones with their horns, you have come too close and should move away immediately.

Musk Ox scat. LG.

Mouflon

Ovis orientalis

The Mouflon comes from Corsica and Sardinia. It has been introduced into nature parks and other captive environments in many places in Europe and has spread in the wild as individuals have escaped. The male, the ram, is larger than the female and has large spiral-shaped horns with deep diagonal grooves.

It is difficult to separate the tracks of deer and Mouflon. Mouflon have long, slender hooves; the front pair is markedly splayed even when moving normally. The hoof is pointed at the front. The hooves are kept close together on the hind legs, and the hind prints are more angular. The ram's tracks are 5.5–6 cm long and 4.5–5 cm wide, the female's somewhat smaller. You can find dew claw prints, but they are very small and very close together, and you can see them only if the animal has moved very fast, has jumped from a significant height, or has moved around in deep snow. The hind foot is placed in the front footprint, the splaying is pronounced, and the stride is very small: for the female 35–40 cm, for the male 40–60 cm.

Mouflon, domestic sheep, and goats will eat bark and branches like deer, and especially in winter, they can remove all the bark. The teeth marks normally appear at somewhat of an oblique angle on the trunk, whereas deer teeth marks often follow the vertical direction of the trunk.

Mouflon gnaw marks on a spruce. AK.

Mouflon scat. EHA.

Mouflon tracks. EHA.

The scat of Mouflon and domestic sheep is 1–2 cm in diameter, compact and angular. The balls of scat often stick together in sausages or clumps 10–15 cm long; the Mouflon scat-balls are somewhat smaller than a sheep's and do not stick together as tightly.

A Mouflon ram. KF.

Chamois

Rupicapra rupicapra/pyrenaica

Chamois are dark brown in winter, and lighter in summer. A Chamois can reach up to 130 cm long and 80 cm at the shoulder; the tail is 10–15 cm long. The face is light with a dark stripe from the mouth to the eyes, as well as a longer and broader stripe on the throat. The small, thick tail is black, the area around the tail light. Both males and females have short horns that kink backwards towards their tips.

The footprints are about 4.5 cm wide and 6.5 cm long; the points of the hooves splay significantly. Prints of the dew claw are visible only in soft terrain, or if the animal has moved very fast. The hind feet are placed towards the leading edge of the front footprints. The stride is 40–70 cm; when the animal jumps, the distance between groups of prints is 150 cm.

The scat is black and spherical, lying in small mounds wherever the animals have passed.

Pyrenean Chamois (pyrenaica) in summer. AG.

Chamois live in mountains at or above the treeline, the females in small herds with the young. Except for the mating season, rams are solitary.

A young Chamois. JBR. Inset: A footprint.

Sheep tracks never show dew claws. EHA.

Sheep scat. EHA.

Domestic sheep

Domestic sheep are normally kept fenced in, but on the Faroe Islands, Iceland, and in the Scottish Highlands, northern Scandinavia, and many small islands, you also find that sheep are more or less free-living animals. Sheep always live in flocks, no matter their size, and you will almost always find hair wherever they have been.

The tracks of sheep resemble those of Roe Deer, but are wider and more rectangular, the front part of the print often significantly rounded; they are 5–6 cm long, 4–5 cm wide, and the prints of the dew claws are never visible.

Rams have spiral horns. Biopix.

Goat scat is smaller than that of sheep.

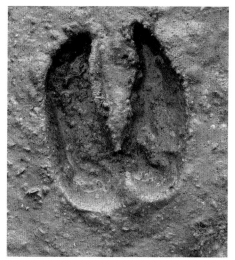

Goat track—always without dew claw prints. EHA.

Goats

Goats are usually tethered or fenced in. The hoof prints are larger than those of sheep, rounded at the ends, and narrower in the front than in back. The front part of the hoof is significantly splayed, 4.5–6 cm wide and up to 3–4.5 cm long. The dew claw leaves no print.

Goats are very agile and can climb into trees and bushes. They can feed extensively on branches and tree trunks.

Goat scat is smaller than that of sheep, cylindrical, about 1 cm in diameter, and flat at the ends.

A herd of domestic goats; both males and females have horns. Biopix.

Two Grey Seals. SS.

The track of a Common Seal in sand. LG.

Seals

You can find eight species of seals on European coastlines. Their tracks are almost identical, and it is practically impossible to tell which species has left them; only their size gives a clue.

Seals move forward with their front flippers; the hind flippers are not used when moving on land, so you see only the tracks of the front flippers and the body as it is dragged across the ground. You find seal tracks on muddy beaches, on sandy soil, and on snow-covered ice.

The front flipper has five toes each with a powerful claw; the prints are very large, about 17 cm wide and about 13 cm long,

and positioned symmetrically across from each other.

The most regularly encountered seal species is **Common Seal**, *Phoca vitulina*.

A Common Seal resting on a rock. AK.

Sea turtles

Two different species of sea turtles breed on the coasts of the Mediterranean: **Loggerhead Turtle**, *Caretta caretta*, and **Green Sea Turtle**, *Chelonia mydas*. Occasionally you can find their tracks on a beach if they have crawled there to lay eggs, normally at night. Sea turtles use only their front flippers when moving on land, and the prints appear as deep holes in the sand but with no claw marks, lying to the side of the broad drag marks left by the shell.

If the turtle is undisturbed, you will find a mound of sand at the end of the tracks that can be up to 0.5 m high and about 1 m in diameter. This is where the turtle has laid its eggs. Before depositing its eggs, the turtle digs a hole about 75 cm deep in the sand with its hind flippers. After the eggs are laid, the hole is covered with powerful movements of the hind flippers, and after about an hour the animal crawls back into the water.

The tracks of the front flippers of Loggerhead Turtle are skewed relative to one another, whereas those of Green Sea Turtle are symmetrical. You may also see drag marks from the tail in the sand, which form a rut.

The track of a Loggerhead Turtle. L-HO.

Turtle tracks can resemble those of a seal, but they are deeper and more splayed, and the drag marks left by the turtle's shell are broader than the marks left by a seal's body.

Sea turtles dig holes in the sand for their eggs. L-HO.

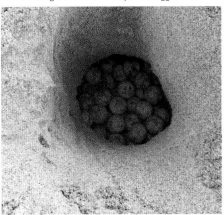

A Loggerhead Turtle on her way back to the sea after laying her eggs. L-HO.

Photo credits

AC – Arthur Christiansen
AD – Adrian Davies/NPL.
AG – Angelo Gandolfi/NPL
AK – Axel Kielland
AL – Alf Linderheim
AT – Anders Tvevad
ATA – Artur Tabor/NPL
AVD – Annemarie van Diepenbeek
BE – Bengt Ekmann
BG – Benny Génsbøl
BL – Bengt Lundberg
BP – Benjamin Pontinen/NPL
BPA – Bill Parker
BPO – Bruno Porlier
BW – Bert Wiklund
BWR – Bob Wright
BZ – Barbara Zerella
CF – Charlie Flemming
CM – Chrissy Marie
DK – David Kjaer/NPL
DN – Dietmar Nill/NPL.
DS – Dagfinn Skjelle
DT – David Tipling/NPL
DW – David Westphalen
EAJ – E.A. Janes
ED – Eric Dragesco
EH – Einar Hugness Hansen
EHA – Elvig Hansen
EM – Erin Michelle
ET – Erik Thomsen
GEH – Gerth Hansen
GH – Göran Hansson
HBH – Hans Bjarne Hansen
HHN – Hans Henrik Nielsen
HJE – Hanne og Jens Eriksen
HN – Heikki Nikki
HP – Harri Pulli
HS – Helge Sørensen
HW – Hugo Willocx/Scanpix

IA – Ingolf Arndt
IK – Ingrid Kielland
ITL – Ib Trap-Lind
JBR – Jose B. Ruix/NPL
JC – John Cancalosi
JH – Jelger Herder
JJ – Jan Johansson
JK – Jens Kirkeby
JKK – Jens Kristian Kjærgaard
J-LK – Jean-Louis Klein
JL – John Larsen
JLI – John Linnel
JORN – J.O. Ravn-Nielsen
JT – Jan Töve
KBA – Kent Bäckström
KF – Kevin Fenlander
KG – Knud Garmann
KH – Kaj Halberg
KHI – Kerstin Hinze/NPL
KR – Klas Rune
KS – Karsten Schnack
LAD – Lars Andreas Dybvik
LGA – Lars Gabrielsson
LG – Lars Gejl
LHL – Lubomir Hlasek
L-HO – Lars-Henrik Olsen
LJ – Lars Jarnemo
LM – Lennart Mathiasson
LS – Lars Serritslev
MDDH – Morten D.D. Hansen
ME – Magnus Elander
MG – Morten Grathe
MH – Mogens Hansen
MLA – Mike Lane
MV – Markus Varesvou
MOF – Magne Ove Furuseth
NO – Niels Olsen
NPHH – Niels Peter Holst Hansen
NPL – © Nature Production/NPL

NWK – Niels Westergaard
    Knudsen
OJ – Ola Jennersten
PB – Preben Bang
PC – Pete Cairns/NPL
PFM – Peter Friis Møller
PH – Pål Hermansson
PN – Peter Nielsen
PW – Peter Weile
RA – Reidar Ansnes
RJS – Reint Jakob Schut/Birdpix,
    NL.
RM – Roy Mangersnes/NN/
    Samfoto
SD – Stephen Dalton/NPL
SDL – Sten Drozd Lund
SJ – Sixten Johnsson
SOJ – Svend Ove Jensen
SS – Søren Skov
SSU – Stig Sunday
ST – Stig Tronvold
TF – Tom Furuseth
TH – Tore Hagmann
THLU – Thomas Lundquist
TJ – Tommi Jacobsson
TL – Tor Lundberg
TLA – Thomas Lazar/NPL
TS – Tim Shepherd/NPL
TSC – Tom Schandy/NN/
    (Samfoto)
TSN – Torben Sten Nielsen
TT – T. Tuoma
UR – Ulf Risberg
VO – Viking Olsson
VS – Vadim Sidorovich/NPL
W – Watson tincap.com
WWE – Wild Wonders of Europe/
    NPL
YS – Yuri Shibnev/NPL

Index of species

(numbers in bold refer to main species accounts)